D1204562

Holy Places of the British Isles

Holy Places of the British Isles

A guide to the legendary and sacred sites

William Anderson

photography by Clive Hicks

LIBRARY
Washington Theological Union
9001 ~~WITHDRAWN~~
Silver Spring, MD 20903-3699

Ebury Press

BL
580
.A53
1983

Acknowledgements The author and photographer and John Calmann & Cooper Ltd are grateful to the following who kindly supplied additional photographs:

Aerofilms Ltd, Boreham Wood: plates 57, 63; Bord Fáilte (the Irish Tourist Board), Dublin: plate 24; Colchester and Essex Museum: plate 61. Plate 45 and plate 101 are reproduced from drawings. All other photographs are by Clive Hicks.

The passages from A. Carmichael, *The Sun Dances: prayers and blessings from the Gaelic* are reproduced by kind permission of the Christian Community Press; those from Tacitus, *The Annals of Imperial Rome*, tr. Grant, and Bede, *A History of the English Church and People*, tr. Sherley-Price, by kind permission of Penguin Ltd; those from K. Hurlestone Jackson, *A Celtic Miscellany*, by kind permission of Routledge and Kegan Paul Ltd.

Published by Ebury Press
National Magazine House
72 Broadwick Street
London W1V 2BP

First impression 1983

Text © 1983 by William Anderson
Photographs © 1983 by Clive Hicks

All rights reserved. No part of this publication may be reproduced, stored in a retrieval system, or transmitted, in any form or by any means, electronic, mechanical, photocopying, recording or otherwise, without prior permission of the publishers.

ISBN 0 85223 266 7

This book was designed and produced by John Calmann and Cooper Ltd, London

Filmset in Great Britain by
Keyspools Ltd, Golborne, Lancs
Printed in Hong Kong by
Mandarin Offset Ltd

1 *Frontispiece* Skellig Michael, off Kerry. Beehive huts built by the monks who lived on this lonely island from *c*. AD 600 onwards, with a view of Little Skellig beyond.

Contents

For John Calmann

Friend and Publisher

The hillside where your ashes rest
Looks down on Arthur's Avalon;
The splendour of your wit, your zest
For life, art, friendship still live on
No more, alas! at your round table
But changed by memory to a golden fable.

But you? the essential you? What cloister
In worlds we're bidden to hereafter
Is tough enough to be your oyster?
What lucky heaven rings with laughter,
Pleased to be mocked by your ripostes,
Proud of a guest who was the prince of hosts?

Chapter 1

The view from Creed Hill: an introduction

Holy places should be seen through the eyes of a child, a lover, or a pilgrim. Then we bring to them perceptions enhanced by the visionary sense that inspired their makers and we are doubly blest for giving as well as receiving. What is deepest and best in our emotions is then opened and made free of the acts of spiritual and artistic greatness that made these places holy.

If I write first of a place that is particularly holy for me it is because it speaks to me with the language of childhood, of affection and of devotion. I think of the top of a hill in Cornwall where I was brought up. It is called Creed Hill because it lies between Creed Church and the village of Grampound. From Creed Hill you look down on the river Fal and its woods and hills and from there you can see, or know that you are close to, sites of nearly all the periods that are considered in this book. Looking north, with the white cones of the claypits on the horizon, you see the Iron Age encampment on Resugga Hill beside one of the Great Western Railway viaducts. Nearer lies the small village of Grampound which has been in decline since the thirteenth century. At that time the silting up of the Fal prevented the ships reaching the quays there for trade that had been continuous with the continent probably long before the time of the Romans. Ptolemy in his *Geography* (*c.* AD 140) called the town by its old name of Volubo— a name that survives alchemically transmuted in the trees on the hills opposite you which are called Golden Woods. In the manor house south of the woods St Cuthbert Mayne, the Jesuit missionary, was hunted down and captured by Queen Elizabeth I's officers to be taken off to Launceston and there hanged, drawn and quartered. Above the woods is the Romano-British trading site of Carvossa. Behind you, several fields away, are the mounds that are all that remain of the manor of Tybesta, granted to his half-brother Robert of Mortain by William the Conqueror as a reward for his part in the defeat of the Saxons whereby the Cornish exchanged one alien ruler for another. A little way down the hill from you under a wych elm is the base of a cross, one of a series set up in the parish by a rector in the fifteenth century, where corpses could rest on their journey to the graveyard at Creed. Though inconveniently placed a mile from the village by way of this steep hill, Creed was so holy a place that the people would not desert it, although later a chapel of ease dedicated to St Nun was built in the village.

Creed was founded by St Crida, the daughter of King Mark, in the sixth century, with the help of a local giant whom she had converted to Christianity. She told him to throw a stone in the air and to build the church wherever the stone fell. A holy well gushes from a hedge in the road beside the graveyard. The present church is of the fourteenth and fifteenth centuries, twin-aisled with its

2 *Above* River Fal, Cornwall. This view, looking towards Trelissick, shows part of the tidal estuary of the river downstream of Creed Hill.

3 *Right* Wells, Somerset. The steps leading (*right*) to the chapter-house of the cathedral and (*left*) to a bridge across a road built for the vicars choral: one of the most famous and atmospheric scenes in English medieval architecture.

south aisle roof thick with heavy wooden roses and leaf bosses. It has a light-filled happy atmosphere to its interior which, in its first days, heard the holy mutter of the mass in Latin and sermons in Cornish and then, from the mid-sixteenth century, the English liturgy and bible which, by inviting participation and understanding from the congregation, helped to drive out the old Cornish language. Charles I's letter of thanks to the Cornish people expressing his lasting gratitude for their support hangs within. Further along the south wall is the tomb inscription of a seventeenth-century vicar, accounted so learned and eloquent that Virgil's epitaph was borrowed as the model for his. It may be translated thus:

> Mylor bore me: Cam taught me: Fal saw my mighty labours;
> Creed now holds my bones buried here.

The churchyard which once abutted the tidal waters of the Fal and now, since the silting, looks down on flat alluvial meadows is poignant with the series of tombs bearing local names, sentinelled by yews, ringed by old trees, and watched by the fine square tower. From there you look across the valley to the hill of Golden Manor where a Roman or Iron Age camp lies under a thick coat of trees and to where, beyond the farms of Grogoth Wartha and Grogoth Wallas, the river floats to the charming but distinctly more modern settlements of Tregony and Ruan Lanihorne.

The religious history of this parish spans a period of three thousand years or more. From such a view as the one I have described, all the elements in its history become omnipresent. They are in fact part of the present landscape

which itself, when more keenly watched and appreciated, reveals its special mood, its atmosphere.

When we speak of a place as being holy, we say something about its innate and acquired atmosphere, its emotional nature.[1] Atmosphere is something only the densest and most self-enclosed of us are insensitive to: it is the mood we appreciate when we enter a room and know, as instantaneously as though we smelled the scent of flowers or rotten eggs, whether the people in it are happy or ill at ease. Houses do not have to be old to possess atmosphere; their aspect, the way light enters them, the nature of the families living in them, all in a very short time help them to acquire an individual feeling. When they have, however, stood for many generations old houses grow about them a mood that is like that of a calm old woman who has outlived her own passions, hatreds, and loves, and has learned to look gently and coolly on the deaths and births of those about her.

Even more powerful is the mood that attaches to many ancient churches. Few houses now lived in are as old as our medieval parish churches such as Creed. Still used for the same purposes of marking the great events of life, a birth, a wedding, a death, and for the cycle of the Christian year, they too seem to have acquired over generations the presence of something serious, something of the hushed moments of the sacraments celebrated in them that affects every stone or piece of wood in their construction and that seems to enter our awareness immediately through the cool ancient smell of their interiors.

Again it is the sum of the emotions expressed and experienced in them that we respond to. Many of these emotions derive from the cycles of life in passing time but there are higher emotions, those for example to which the contemplative life and the civilizing arts aspire and from which they draw their nourishment. The distinction between the different atmospheres of passing time and the eternal world is one that is frequently stressed in the following pages and though hard to express is an important one. A way of putting it is to compare Thomas Gray's *Elegy in a Country Churchyard*, written about Stoke Poges, where the powerful emotions he expresses are all drawn from the spectacle of the generations each declining into death, with another more recent poem, Eliot's *Little Gidding*. There Eliot speaks of 'the intersection of the timeless moment', signifying the cognition of other and higher states of consciousness and the interpenetration of life by the eternal world.

Yet another way of putting it is this. If an old church, saturated in the generations of emotions expressed within and about it, can strike the visitor with so powerful a sense of atmosphere, then what of the power associated with the places which were the scenes of new spiritual movements and new civilizations? A lonely old church, a ruined priory, a broken-down chapel of ease, may possess strong atmosphere, but these buildings only exist because of spiritual and civilizing events that may have taken place far from their localities and which transcend the concerns of parochial patriotism. The view from Creed Hill is good to start from, but the view of West Kennet and Silbury from Overton Sanctuary, the view of Canterbury Cathedral from the Pilgrims' Way, the view from the summit of Croagh Patrick, all bring us much closer to the points of beginning in our civilization and the constant remaking of humanity.

Such places are associated with great happenings in history; they are windows in the house of time through which new ideas and new attitudes to nature glance in and ensure that settled patterns of existence must change for ever. These are changes of the order of the introduction of farming in the

4 Glendalough, Wicklow. The upper lake beside which St Kevin, the founder of the monastery here, used to retire. (*See page 87*)

Neolithic period, one of the biggest revolutions in the history of humanity; of the series of invasions between 700 BC and AD 500 which brought to these islands a succession of races including the La Tène Celts, the Belgae, the Romans, and the Anglo-Saxons; of the introduction of Christianity and of the major upheavals and changes within the Church from the martyrdom of St Alban to the Reformation and the movements thereafter. To appreciate the atmosphere of the places associated with such events we have to think on the scale of thousands or of millions of beings at one time, of their yearnings, fears, and emotions stirred by the release of great energies both through natural disturbances such as a major climatic change and by the movement of distant peoples or the fall of empires. These times of change in history are also the times when, countering or channelling the energies released, new religions and new civilizations can enter and transform the possibilities of life for mankind.

The word 'holy' carries within its history and its associations many of these changes. It comes from the Anglo-Saxon word 'halig' which describes something that must be kept complete or inviolate. It has the connotations of wholeness and unity. The Anglo-Saxons, who shared the religious beliefs of the Scandinavians and the North Germans, would have applied it to their sacred groves and their wooden sanctuaries and temples adorned with horse skulls and the trophies of war. Driven from their terpens, or settlements, in North Germany by pressure from tribes from the east and by wide-scale flooding and the rising of the water level, they successfully invaded Britain, bringing their own religious customs with them and for long remaining impervious to the largely Christianized society of Roman Britain which they overwhelmed. When they did accept Christianity, 'halig' was the word already prepared for the translation of the Latin Christian concepts of *sacer* and *sanctus*. *Sanctus* has given us 'saint' and 'sanctuary' but also, when translated as holy, it appears in the third person of the Trinity, *Spiritus Sanctus*, as the Holy Ghost. The sense of unity was conveyed in the related words 'hallow' and 'hallowed', a hallow being a holy place, and 'hallowed', surviving chiefly in the first petition of the Lord's Prayer when we ask to be made one with 'Thy name'. The sense of wholeness also appears in other etymological cousins of 'holy', as in 'hale' and 'health', with reference to our physical well-being. St Paul said that we should regard our bodies as the Temple of the Holy Ghost[2]—and we will, among the holy places described here, come across many examples of buildings and sites deliberately designed to expand our awareness of the human form into an ideal of what man or woman can attain, as in the basing of the design of churches on the form of the Body of Christ.

A word of the importance of 'holy' may have a great beginning but it acquires the many levels of meaning that give it especial associative power through the understanding and direct experience of the men and women who express its meaning. Similarly, with a holy place which may be naturally endowed with remarkable features such as, for example, the rock of Durham entoured by the river Wear, it needs the presence of holy men and women for it to acquire its special atmosphere. Our conventional idea of holiness is limited perhaps to the saints and monks and nuns of the Dark Ages and the Middle Ages, but here I want to make use of the association of concepts of wholeness and unity with holiness to paint a wider picture, to include in it not only the saint lying in his shrine but the artists and architects who made that shrine, to celebrate those of whatever religion or cult who added to the wholeness of experience of their contemporaries and their descendants by their ability to heal them in the spirit,

5 Fountains Abbey, North Yorkshire. A view of the east end of the abbey ruins showing the chapel of the nine altars and the tower, with the river Skell in the foreground. (*See page 127*)

the mind, or the body and to give them delight through their art or poetry. The making of a holy place begins as an event in the souls of men—as a spiritual event of understanding and illumination that drives them to seek those places whose natural features correspond to and mirror the needs of their inner lives. In this way, a small band of monks fled the distracting comforts of St Mary's Abbey at York to find a wild and obscure valley where they began and established Fountains Abbey in surroundings that perfectly answered the demands of the Cistercian rule. In a not dissimilar way Wordsworth, having explored the world in a time of revolution and unrest, returned to his native Cumberland to write the works that have permanently changed men's view of Nature, landscape, and the development of the poet's soul. Or to give an example from far earlier times, Neolithic men would seem to have especially associated

6 *Below left* Carrowmore, Sligo. A chambered tomb with Ben Bulben in the distance. Carrowmore contains the largest concentration of megalithic monuments in Ireland.

whiteness with the Great Goddess (otherwise known as the White Goddess) and often to have chosen stones that contained veins of white quartz for their megalithic monuments: the chalk downlands of Wiltshire must therefore have seemed a particularly propitious place for their holy places and, in clearing the forests there for agriculture, it must have been as though they were discovering the signature of their deity in the soil they laid bare.

Over the centuries various abiding or recurring features of the face of the earth have acquired significance as emblems of the states and moods of the psyche. To the child, the lover, and the visionary, everything is alive and to them all landscapes are landscapes of the soul. To what was said earlier in affirmation of the emotional nature of atmosphere it can be objected that every thought and feeling we experience in a place or landscape is something we bring to it ourselves. We are projecting our own associations, fears, hopes, and capacity for awe into the place. At a shallow personal level this may often be true, but the purpose of holy places is to open us up to wider and more universal experiences. One way in which many holy places work this change in us is through the particular symbolism of their landscapes, which either by their natural features or with the help of conscious art are expressions of great archetypes living in the depths of our souls. Let us take some of the most simple and powerful features of the face of the earth—the sea, rivers, wells and springs, trees, groves, woods, downs, hills, and mountains—and see how they relate to the holy places found amongst them and how they enhance the significance of these places.

Since the submergence of the last land links with continental Europe in about 7000 BC and the creation of the Channel, all invaders and immigrants have had

7 *Below* The sea as an image of creation: a wave caught in the moment of breaking on the Anglesey coast at sunset.

to cross the sea to reach the British Isles. The sea is at once the barrier and the means of transmission of the new. Of all earth's surface the sea is the part least affected by man and the element that most continuously reminds him of his smallness in the face of the vast energies of the universe. The immensity of the sea compels man to seek a comforter and a helper in the creator of those energies. Thus the fishermen of Barra, southernmost island of the Outer Hebrides, would sing:

Father! O Son! O Spirit Holy!
Be thou, Three-One, with us day and night
And on the back of the wave as on the mountainside
Our Mother shall be with us with her arm under our head.[3]

8 St Govan's Chapel, Dyfed. The thirteenth-century chapel built on the site of St Govan's cell of the sixth century, in a cleft of the cliffs below Trevailon Downs. The niche where St Govan hid from persecutors may also be seen.

The waves of the sea are emblems both of the inconstancy of human fortune and of creation: from Neolithic times into the Middle Ages the wave symbol, called in heraldry the chevron, has been a reiterated image.

The margins of the sea have their own meaning and significance as the meeting-place of the elements. Great significance was attached by the Iron Age builders of hillforts to promontories jutting out into the sea such as the Dodman

9 Inishmurray, Sligo. Beehive cells with a complete cashel wall of an early Christian monastery set on an island with, in the distance, Ben Bulben, the mountain which W. B. Yeats often wrote about. The monastery suffered badly in the ninth-century Viking raids.

in Cornwall or Harlech, the seat of Bran the Blessed. These headlands were giant expressions of the image of the human head or skull, so important in Celtic myth and religion. The Celtic and Anglo-Saxon monks who followed them not only built monasteries on wild headlands such as Tintagel or tidal islands such as Lindisfarne or the Brough of Birsay in Orkney, but also favoured far-out and almost inaccessible islands such as the Skelligs off the south-west coast of Ireland or Bardsey off the coast of Wales. The island is a place of concentration and solitude; it symbolizes the enclosed nature of the soul given to God or, as in the earlier use of the Isles of Scilly as the Islands of the Dead, of the soul returned home after life.

Turning inland we find that a related symbolism attaches to the river as the image of the flow of time and human lives. As the chief means of communication between the interior and the world outside, many rivers are rich in holy places along their banks. Up the Shannon, for example, we find a succession of cathedrals and monasteries, from Scattery on an island at its mouth, up to Limerick, Killaloe, Clonfert, and Clonmacnois; or along the Thames from Westminster Abbey up to St Frideswide's shrine at Oxford, passing many ancient sites and monasteries. Thus the Cavalier poet Sir John Denham, writing

10 *Above* Tintagel, Cornwall. A view from the site of the Celtic monastery on this headland, which has many associations with Arthurian legend.

11 *Left* Priestholm or Puffin Island, Anglesey. The island as a symbol of the solitude of the soul dedicated to God. St Seiriol founded a hermitage here in the sixth century.

of the ancient sites beside its banks of Windsor Castle and Chertsey Abbey, could describe the Thames as:

Hasting to pay his tribute to the sea
Like mortal life to meet Eternity,

and the image of communication is powerfully conveyed in Denham's apostrophe to the river:

O could I flow like thee, and make thy stream
My great example, as it is my theme!
Though deep, yet clear, though gentle, yet not dull,
Strong without rage, without o'er-flowing full.[4]

12 *Below* The Isles of Scilly. The Old Man of the Gugh: a standing stone on a small tidal island next to St Agnes. The exceptional number of prehistoric burial sites on the Isles of Scilly confirms their reputation as the Islands of the Dead.

13 *Overleaf* Eskdale, Cumbria. Lakeland mountains seen above a valley. The mountain is one of the most potent symbols of spiritual challenge and attainment in many religions and traditions.

Calm water, as in a still lake, symbolizes the stilled mind reflecting the nature of God, and much power in popular superstition attaches to wells and springs which are still thought to be able to heal or to grant wishes. Water in Christian ritual is the means of transmission of grace and salvation in baptism and therefore of rebirth and the regeneration of the soul.

The forest or wood has long signified the human mind or often the dark places of the human psyche. Clearings in groves or woods were especially sacred to the Celtic Druids and the clumps of beeches that still crown many ancient hilltop sites such as Chanctonbury Ring or Wittenham Clumps on the Sinodun Hills possess a powerful dreaming atmosphere. The powers of the forest, the place of everything wild and unregenerate, as opposed to the reason of the city and the open farmland, were to be expressed in the intertwined monsters and vegetation of Romanesque sculpture and then to be redeemed and transfigured in the very

14 *Above* Rydal Water, Cumbria. The still lake reflecting like a looking-glass is a symbol of the pure soul mirroring God.

15 *Left* Dunadd, Argyll. The seat of power of the Scotic kings of Dalriada where St Columba came in the course of his mission to Scotland. The site was occupied from the late fifth century until the Vikings settled here in the ninth century.

16 *Right* Holne Chase, Dartmoor. The wood is an ancient emblem of the mind.

forms of Gothic columns and vaulting, its vegetation crowning the capitals and garlanded in the screens and bosses.

In many ways the most powerful image is that of the mountain—man's own soul and the ascent every man must take.[5] Hills and mountains, whether we look at them from below, or, better still, climb them, give us a sense of liberation because they help us to see ourselves within a bigger scale. The mountain appears in the symbolism of most great religions and philosophies. In the *Bhagavad Gita*, when the Lord Krishna says 'I am Meru among mountains', he is referring to the mythical mountain of Hindu tradition which is a seven-sided pyramid of gold situated at the North Pole and whose seven facets flash with the colours of the rainbow. When seen as a whole, Meru blazes pure white, signifying unity and the purity of consciousness.

The symbolism of the mountain has a twofold nature. The outside of the mountain concerns the living while the inside may contain the land of the dead, or the place where vanished races and heroes of the past have fled or lie in slumber. Thus the Sidhe, the heroic fairy race of Ireland, live within the raths or ancient hillforts, or in the mountains themselves. Many are the hills where Arthur is said to sleep and from which he and his knights have been seen to issue. One of the chief functions of the monasteries was to provide a continuous service of prayer for the dead and thereby to experience in this life a foretaste of the communion of saints, and in the choice of wild hilly sites such as Llanthony or Fountains the monks may well have been aware of ancestral traditions drawing them to these places.

If the interior of the mountain concerns the past, the dead, and other non-human races, then its outer face provides innumerable analogies for the trials

17 *Above* River Wye, Gwent. A great river symbolizes in its journey to the sea the life of man and the return of his soul to its creator. As a means of navigation it also provides an image of communication.

18 *Right* Scattery, Clare. The round tower and the small ruined cathedral set on a tiny island in the mouth of the Shannon. The name Scattery comes from a monster overcome by St Senan, who founded a monastery here in the sixth century.

and achievements of this life and for our mental sufferings and tribulations:

> O the mind, mind has mountains; cliffs of fall
> Frightful, sheer, no-man-fathomed. Hold them cheap
> May who ne'er hung there[6]

wrote Gerard Manley Hopkins. The theme of the ascent of a mountain recurs again and again in mystical writings concerned with some form of initiation or with the journey of the soul to God. It is thought that in pre-Christian days Glastonbury Tor, that strange hill rising out of the flat surrounding plain now drained of its lake, was the focus of a maze pattern followed by the seekers of past ages on a journey of initiation. Later consecrated to St Michael, of whose church only the tower now remains on its summit, the Tor was included in the round of

19 Llanthony, Powys. The ruins of the Augustinian abbey set in the Black Mountains. It was originally founded in the late eleventh century by a knight who, while hunting, took refuge in a ruined chapel here during a storm and underwent a conversion.

holy sites associated with Joseph of Arimathaea and the great abbey of Glastonbury. The link with the Archangel Michael shows it to have been considered a place where some great evil was once overcome. It is part of the chain of mountains or precipitous islands across Europe devoted to the same patron, from Monte Gargano in Italy to Mont St Michel off the French coast and to St Michael's Mount in Cornwall.

The summit of the mountain has very special significances of its own: by ancient tradition it is the place of the propitiation of the gods. The St Andrew's Cross, the saltire of Scotland, may be seen as an expression of the mountain summit where the earth, rising up to the point of the crossing, meets the inverted cone of the influences of heaven descending to man.

In old Celtic belief it was held that on Easter Day the sun dances for joy. In the last century Alexander Carmichael wrote down and translated from the Gaelic this description by an old lady, Barbara Macphie of Dreimsdale, of what she saw one Easter morning from the summit of Benmore:

The glorious gold-bright sun was after rising on the crests of the great hills, and it was changing colour—green; purple, red, blood-red, white, intense-white, and gold-white, like the glory of the God of the elements to the children of men. It was dancing up and down in exultation at the joyous resurrection of the beloved Saviour of Victory.

To be thus privileged, a person must ascend to the top of the highest hill before sunrise, and believe that the God who makes the small blade of grass to grow is the same God who makes the large, massive sun to move.[7]

Much of the various symbolism of the mountain is linked into one appealing and still vital legend, the story of St Patrick and his conversion of Ireland, especially in his travels from Slane to Tara and then to Lough Crew and Croagh Patrick.[8] We must ignore the labours of scholars who have tried to divide the St Patrick of legend into at least two and even more St Patricks, because our St Patrick is the brave young man who in the fifth century was captured by pirates and taken from Britain to Ireland where he was sold as a slave. He escaped back to Britain but was seized by the desire to bring Christianity to Ireland with its inviolate Celtic pagan society and religion. Ireland had long been ruled by local kings under the sovereignty of a high king whose seat was at Tara.

Tara, as one approaches it through country roads, offers little promise of the spectacular. You climb over a stile into a green field curving gently upwards and walk to the top, where you suddenly find yourself on an immense elevated plain mounded with the remains of fallen buildings that go back to the Bronze Age. And then you understand why it was chosen by the kings and named Tara of the Kings because for miles around all the neighbouring hills look towards it, most notably the Hill of Slane on the northern banks of the river Boyne.

It was on the Hill of Slane that St Patrick chose to challenge the power of the druid priests of old Ireland and to wrest from them the guiding relationship they had maintained with the secular rulers. It was Easter Saturday in the year AD 433. It was the custom that no fire or light should be lit until the kindling of the royal fire at Tara, visible for miles around. To the druids' horror they saw a rebel fire lit on the Hill of Slane leaping higher and higher, the Paschal fire lit by Patrick. They pointed out this fire to the High King and told him that unless the fire on the Hill of Slane was extinguished that night, it would never be quenched in Ireland. St Patrick refused to listen to messages bidding him put it out, and the High King and the druids had to travel in their chariots to Slane to bring him back to Tara. Their attempts failed when the King ordered his men to seize

20 *Left, above* Rock of Cashel, Tipperary. The cathedral, castle, and round tower seen above the perimeter wall on the imposing site where St Patrick began the conversion of Munster. (*See page 86*)

21 *Left, below* Glastonbury Tor, Somerset. A natural mound carved with a spiral path of ascent about it which some have said was a ritual path of initiation going back to the Bronze Age. (*See pages 79–82*)

22 *Above* Slane, Meath. Here St Patrick lit the Paschal fire, the deed that challenged the power of the ancient druid cults of Ireland. The ruin is a nineteenth-century Gothick folly.

Patrick. The saint uttered in a loud cry, 'Let God arise!', and the men fought one another, leaving the King and his family to return to Tara.

The next day, Easter Day, St Patrick with five companions suddenly appeared before the King and his court in the great banqueting-hall whose traces still can be followed down the north-eastern side of Tara. Challenged with his crime of lighting a fire before that of the King, he spoke of the spiritual meaning of fire and of the light of Christ. A druid tried to poison him; he blessed the cup, the liquid congealed so that the poison could be poured out, then it liquefied again, and he drank the remaining contents unharmed. A dramatic contest then took place between Patrick and the druids in which their magic was always defeated by the higher power (and greater efficiency) of his miracles.

Having survived and conquered on the Hills of Slane and Tara Patrick now set out westward, his aim the centre of druid power and worship at Mag Slecht, 'the place of prostration', on a high limestone shelf near Lough Crew. Here was the idol of Crom Cruach on which Patrick advanced brandishing his staff and uttering a loud shout, at which the idol collapsed. This place, which still retains its monoliths and stone circles, was said to have been one of human sacrifice and also one where the druids kept their cursing or maledictive stones—no more since Patrick.

The last hill he had to conquer is one of the most remarkable sites of all those considered in this book. It is the mountain of Croagh Patrick, a cone of quartzite rising 2,500 ft from the southern side of Clew Bay on the Atlantic Coast. Here his enemies were not idolatry or the spells of 'women and smiths and druids' against which he invokes the Trinity in his prayer known as the 'Breast-plate', but what he calls in the same prayer 'every demon's snare' and 'every savage force that may come upon me, body and soul'. He chose this mountain, whose triangular shape is like a symbol of the Trinity, for an exorcism of demonic forces and for a claim on Heaven for the protection of Ireland. He intended to spend Lent in the year 441 there.

He ascended the mountain and spent forty days and nights in prayer on the tiny plateau at its summit, assailed by dark forces and by demons in the shape of black birds clamouring and wheeling about him. Then they departed routed and angels came to minister to him and to ask him what he desired. His request, that Ireland should keep the faith till the Last Coming, appalled them. Three times the angels refused, begging him to ask for something less; on the fourth occasion they conceded and told him his prayer would be granted. At that he arose and hurled his bell many times down the great chasm known as Lugnagoul on the

north-east side of the mountain. The angels would catch it as it reached the bottom and throw it back to him, until by this exercise all the demons and noisome spirits and beasts and reptiles were driven from Ireland.

Behind this legend must lie the reality of a tremendous act of transformation, first within Patrick himself and then, as a result, in Irish pagan society under the impact of Christianity. For all the descriptions of them in the legends as demonic and idolatrous, the ancient Irish beliefs had enormous vitality in them; although their practice may have fallen into a degenerate state by the time of Patrick's mission, much that was good in them and much that was stable in Irish social and political life was adapted to Christian uses and the creation of a civilization that was to have incalculable effects on the preservation of learning and religion in the rest of Europe in the Dark Ages.

23 *Above left* Tara, Meath. The Stone of Destiny which shrieked when touched by the chariot wheels of a high king of Ireland, standing on the high plateau of Tara. Here St Patrick, after lighting the Paschal fire, won his contest with the druids.

24 *Above* Croagh Patrick, Mayo. A view of the mountain of St Patrick seen from the shore of Clew Bay.

The legend of Croagh Patrick incorporates an exceptional number of the aspects of the symbolism of the mountain—in the ardours and difficulties of Patrick's ascent and vigil against the demons, in his baring of his soul on the naked summit and his perseverance against the angels' refusal of his request, and in his exorcism of the dark inner side of the mountain, the demons and beasts that represent the old, the dead, the decayed that hinder the development of the soul. Such is the power of the place and its associations that it is now the main pilgrimage site devoted to St Patrick. Over 80,000, it is said, climb the mountain on the last Sunday in July, many in bare feet and some on their knees. They proceed by three stations, the first called after St Brendan, where the pilgrims recite seven *Paters*, seven *Aves*, and one *Credo*, while making seven clockwise circuits. These prayers are repeated at the second station on the

summit, called Patrick's bed, where there is a modern chapel, and then at the third, dedicated to the Virgin, on a western ridge.

My own ascent was made, not on the pilgrimage day, but still, suitably, in March in the period of Lent which was the time of Patrick's vigil. It had been snowing and the streams running down the scree were frozen over; and though I did not take off my shoes, they were so thin it would have made little difference. My companions were two physicists, one of whom, a young Greek called Nikkos, we soon left behind; the other, a Canadian, had lungs of iron, a sceptical attitude, and a fluency in conversation in steep places that had me begging for mercy, so little breath did I have even for minimal response. We followed a heather-lined stream up to the first steep ascent to a col stretching out eastwards from the mountain. The slipperiness of the ice, the sinister face of Lugnagoul on our right, the fear of falling, all made me want to give up many times and only the urgings of my companion, who pointed out I had suggested the ascent in the first place, shamed me into continuing. Then suddenly we were on a flat ridge, rewarded by the views to the south of the Connemara mountains, their dark blue and purple snow-grained and peaked, across an immense valley of brown heather. We swung along easily and happily until we reached the real ascent of the cone of the mountain itself, and any difficulties I had experienced before

25 *Above* Carrawburgh, Cumbria. The temple of Mithras, established after about AD 205 for soldiers serving on the nearby Hadrian's Wall. It was probably desecrated by Christians about a hundred years later. (*See page 76*)

26 *Right* A modern pilgrim climbing Croagh Patrick in the mist.

were as nothing to what I now faced. It was not surprising that some prefer to go up on their knees; the ascent is so steep that I had to bend forward to keep my balance on the sharp stones and my knees were almost touching the mountain all the time. My sturdier companion went on ahead because I could only make five steps at a time without resting. We were now on the south side of the mountain, having spiralled round from the north where we began. The sun was on us and every now and then further views were revealed by the ascent, till suddenly there was the Atlantic blazing and twinkling as though it were being beaten by the hammers of invisible goldsmiths. Again and again I wanted to give up and my body became a dogged automaton. Then at last I was climbing through snow, encouraged by shouts from above, and, amazed, found I was on the summit. At first my head was still so accustomed to being bent down low that I only noticed what was before my feet, and I was startled by an amazing sight: the snow had been driven in long ridges by the wind careering over the summit and it must have been so cold that the snow had been frozen on the point of being blown off, so that on the further end of the ridges flowered marvellous crystals with flakes like petals. Then, daring, I raised my head to take in the view the summit afforded, the three hundred islands of Clew Bay, the mountain of Nephin Beg beyond it, the islands of Achill and Clare and the Atlantic around and beyond, and the purple mountains of the south. On the way down we met our other friend Nikkos whom we had left behind so far below. My companion, who had been so loud in his denunciations of religion on the ascent, then performed a Christian act beyond both my strength and my imagination: he turned back immediately to escort Nikkos to the top. I descended, alone, in a state of proud humility, knowing with delight it would take me months to assimilate the beauty and the meaning of the experience.

If my description of the difficulties of the ascent may seem exaggerated, the sceptical reader should turn to other accounts. They are mostly by clerics and therefore undoubtedly true—and I had an easy time by comparison. One result of my climb was that, if ever I mentioned in Ireland that I had climbed Croagh Patrick, a new warmth would immediately enter into my reception, and I saw more deeply into the emotional meaning that the mountain still holds for the Irish. Oliver St John Gogarty, writing of an ascent in the thirties, remarks on much the same experience: 'I was popular,' he says, 'and through no fault of my own.'[9]

Chapter 2

The Earth as Mother: Neolithic and Bronze Age sites

27 New Grange, Louth. Part of the rebuilt façade of quartzite stones embedded with sea-rounded stones, with kerb-stones at the base that ring the mound. In the distance the outlying stones form part of the henge circle.

The source of the River Boyne, according to ancient Irish legend, is the well belonging to the gods who are ruled by their mother Dana; the well contains five salmon and is surrounded by the nine hazel trees of wisdom. The nuts containing all knowledge drop into the water and are eaten by the salmon; the colour of the nuts then appears in red spots in the scales of the salmon. Any man or woman who can catch and eat even a small part, even a scale, of one of those salmon, acquires all wisdom and the knowledge of poetry. The legend expresses the ancient belief that wisdom and inspiration are concentrated in special places and arise through the waters and the plants issuing from the earth. In a similar way the image of Earth as Mother, producing from her womb not only crops, cattle, men and women, stones, minerals, and forests, but also the knowledge and guidance to make all these fruitful or useful, may be considered the

dominant symbol in the holy places of the Neolithic and Bronze Age periods.[1] It was she who inspired the Neolithic farmers living further down the river at the Brugh na Bóinne (the bend in the Boyne) to create in the fourth millennium BC the earliest of the holy places to be considered here in detail: the great mound of New Grange.

New Grange is one of three notable passage graves grouped closely together on the banks of the Boyne. Their builders are thought to have links with the Almerian culture in Spain: there were certainly exchanges between Ireland and Spain at this date. What the visitor first sees is a vast mound looming at the top of a field. The mound is over 240 ft across and 30 ft high and the side containing the entrance is faced with white quartz embedded with sea-rounded boulders, the size of cannonballs. Both quartz and boulders were brought many miles from

28 New Grange. The passage, showing the huge slabs with which it is lined.

30 *Page 38* Castlerigg, Cumbria. A stone circle surrounded by lakeland mountains which has attracted much scientific interest because of its astronomical alignments.

separate sites on the coastline of the Irish sea. The present façade is a restoration, using the thousands of pieces of quartz discovered in the course of excavations. The entrance itself is original. Immediately before it lies an immense stone carved with triple spirals, circles, lozenges and other shapes. Skirting this threshold stone you enter the portal which carries a window or light box over its lintel. You pass through the 60-ft-long passage with standing stones inclining at what seem odd angles, noting yet more lozenge and spiral patterns, until you reach the chamber at the end with its three recesses or chapels and its corbelled roof. On the end wall of the recess facing the entrance are three spiral patterns and it is these patterns that help to bring out the significance of this site. It was discovered in 1969 that the passage is so aligned that the light of sunrise can pass through the window or light box over the entrance and strike the end wall,

29 New Grange. A view of the entrance showing the light box through which the sun enters at the winter solstice and, in front, the portal stone carved with spirals, lozenges, and (*bottom right*) chevrons.

illuminating these spirals, only on the winter solstice and a few days before and after that date. This discovery revealed that New Grange was not only an immense burial mound containing 200,000 tonnes of stones—and one of the world's most important repositories of Neolithic art—but also that it was an astronomical clock for determining the time of midwinter. The spirals, the eye shapes (oculi) and the chevron patterns are all linked with examples from many other countries connected with the worship of the Great Mother Goddess. The deliberate use of the white quartzite facing also connects with her as the White Goddess and the ritual significance of the alignment of the passage to the winter solstice may have centred on the hope of rebirth, of renewal of life and growth as the sun's rays penetrated into the depths of the mound,[2] which is a depiction of her at once in her bridal aspect through the ring of stones surrounding the mound, her birth aspect in the pregnant shape of the mound, and in her death aspect as a burial chamber.

The discovery of the New Grange solstitial alignment was one of several discoveries in the past twenty years which started to confirm the exceptional geometric skills and astronomical knowledge of prehistoric society in this period.[3] New Grange is dated 3300 BC, a thousand years before the construction of the sarsen circles of Stonehenge, probably the most complex of all the monuments now thought to act as astronomical clocks or computers. These new studies have transformed our conceptions of what society must have been like in those times.

A diffusion of the influences from the New Grange culture would have appeared to have spread to Wales. The most important comparable sites in Great Britain are in the Orkneys and Wessex, to which we will come soon. First,

31 Swinside, Cumbria. A circle of 55 stones in a remote site at the head of the Furness peninsula.

32 Pentre Ifan, Dyfed. A notable cromlech on a ridge commanding the Nevern valley.

however, it would be helpful to look backwards in time from the vantage point of New Grange. Already long before the time of New Grange, the hunting communities in which men—possibly from the earliest days—had lived had been superseded by a society of more settled farmers. We can know little of the religion and rites of the early hunters. Unlike France and Spain, in the British Isles there are no certain or authentic cave paintings such as those at Lascaux or Altamira (29000 BC). The burial of a young man who had been painted with red ochre and wearing a necklace of wolf and reindeer teeth in Paviland, a cave in Pembrokeshire, is one of the few pieces of evidence on which to base attitudes to religion and death for thousands of years. Engravings on bones from upper Palaeolithic caves and the antler frontlets or masks probably used in ritual dances from the later site of Star Carr in Yorkshire are all we have of art for the same kind of period. With the Neolithic period, however, and the beginnings of farming in the British Isles between 5000 and 4000 BC we start to find many more reliable ritual and religious sites. These farmers were the makers of megalithic culture, the builders of monuments of 'great stones'; they shared their culture with many communities on the continent, most notably in Iberia and in Brittany where the alignments of Carnac remain as one of the most impressive of their achievements.

Among the earliest of their ritual sites are the long barrows and dolmens and the causewayed camps. Many of these appear to have been in use either for burial or for ritual purposes over very long periods—a thousand years in some cases. In the case of the long barrow known as Wayland's Smithy near the Ridgeway on the Berkshire downs, excavations have shown that the first construction on the site was a wooden mortuary house for the storage of corpses

33 *Above* Avebury, Wiltshire. Giant stones of the south-west circle looking towards the entrance to the henge from the Kennet avenue.

34 *Left* Maeshowe, Orkney. The interior of the greatest chambered tomb in Europe, showing the skilfully laid drystone masonry and part of the corbelling of the roof.

35 *Right* Stonehenge, Wiltshire. The most famous of all megalithic monuments, Stonehenge was built in three main stages between 2800 and 1600 BC.

which had already been allowed to decompose in the open air. This house was covered by a low mound later disturbed by the erection of a chambered tomb of upright stones.

The dolmens or cromlechs which consist in their most characteristic form of three upright stones bearing an immense capstone like a tabletop are equally intriguing. They have been described as the first architecture. To stand and look at one of these immense and mysterious erections, instinct as they are with primeval symbolism, can be a deeply moving experience. Such a one is the cromlech of Pentre Ifan standing on the north slopes of the Prescelly mountains on the borders of Pembrokeshire and Cardiganshire.

The third type of ritual site is the causewayed camp, the earliest of which to be dated is Hembury Camp in Devon, about 4000 BC. Originally these camps were thought to be fortifications but the immense areas they cover and the wide gaps or causeways in their earthen or chalk walls, combined with a recognition of the small populations available either to attack or defend them, has brought about the realization that they probably combined the functions of ritual sites and trading centres. One of the most important of these is Windmill Hill near Avebury. The earliest signs here are of pits into which ritual offerings were put, dated to about 3000 BC. The way these pits are arranged reveals patterns on the ground that have been interpreted[4] as depictions of the Goddess. Later, in about 2750 BC, three concentric ditches covering an area of about 21 acres were dug and the deposits here revealed rich finds of bones and artefacts. The site was in use for hundreds of years.

What these three types of construction reveal to us is a concern for the dead and a belief in the existence of a world beyond death, the use of stone in the construction of ritual or holy places and, in the case of Windmill Hill and other causewayed camps, a desire to mould and remake the landscape on a grand scale. The most remarkable combination of these elements was to be erected quite close to Windmill Hill in the complex of the West Kennet long barrow, Silbury Hill, Overton Sanctuary and Avebury.

These are the greatest monuments of Wessex of the period and indeed of the whole British Isles. The chalk downland of Wiltshire, wherever the modern traveller looks, bears the evidence of the labour of Neolithic and Bronze Age men to sculpt and mould it into significant and symbolic forms. The very whiteness of the chalk, revealed wherever a sod was overturned, would remind them of the White Goddess. They tried to make the earth on which they depended for their crops and the sustenance of their animals a harmonious extension of their own human form by carving the landscape into sculptures of the Goddess. The continuity of their society or at least of traditions that could be handed on from generation to generation or from one race or tribe to another meant that this labour of re-forming and giving emphasis to features of the landscape was a duty and a delight that gave inspiration over hundreds of years. It has been recently pointed out that what the Wessex landscape sculptors were doing has a parallel in the ancient Chinese practice of Feng-shui, the deliberate changing of features of the landscape so as to make it propitious and more fruitful according to the rules and symbolism of the Chinese theory of five elements and the balance to be achieved between the green dragon of the hills and the blue tiger of the valleys.[5] Similarly, but basing their symbolism on the worship of the Great Goddess and on her relationship with the fertilizing Sun, the men and women of the Neolithic and Bronze Age found in the evocative shapes of the downland an environment that impelled them to shape and shovel and dig to make works of art that at the

36 *Top* Silbury, Wiltshire.
A view of the greatest
man-made hill of antiquity
in Europe, Silbury Hill,
seen from the causewayed
camp of Windmill Hill.
According to the
interpretation followed in
the text, the purpose of
Silbury was as a harvest
hill sacred to the Great
Goddess. It symbolizes the
Goddess pregnant.

37 *Right* Silbury Hill, seen
across a cornfield from the
West Kennet Long Barrow
which may have been a
site connected with the
Great Goddess in her death
aspect.

38 *Left, above* Callanish, Isle of Lewis. The stones seen under a full moon.

39 *Left, below* Ring of Brodgar, Orkney. Set between two lochs on an isthmus, the stones of the Ring of Brodgar are aligned with significant astronomical events.

40 *Above* Merry Maidens, Cornwall. Seen here in a Cornish mist, these stones, according to legend, were once girls turned to stone for dancing on a Sunday.

41 *Right* Stonehenge, Wiltshire. Druids performing their midsummer rites. This was taken shortly before sunrise on the occasion described on page 63.

same time rendered the land more fertile, provided them with accurate calendrical information, and satisfied them with the expression of their deepest impulses.

The earliest of the sites in the Avebury complex is the West Kennet long barrow begun in about 3250 BC and completed in about 2600 BC with the sealing of the burial chambers and the erection of the great portal stones that may symbolize the sacred ox. The barrow itself is an immense trapezoid, a shape that according to the same symbolism signifies the aspect of the Goddess as hag or death. The chambers inside are separated by sarsen stones linked with fine drystone walling. They once contained over forty skeletons—or rather incomplete skeletons because certain bones had been removed for ritual purposes.

The path up to the barrow passes through a field at the corner of which can be seen the source of the river Kennet, the Swallowhead which is of great importance for the interpretation of the next site. Silbury Hill is the largest man-made mound erected in Europe in prehistory. Its base covers $5\frac{1}{2}$ acres and its truncated top rises 150 ft above the fields about it. A legend recorded by John Aubrey says that it was raised while a posset of milk was seething. Another story says it contains the gold statue of a king on horseback. Later researchers chose to regard it as a gigantic Bronze Age barrow, the equivalent for some Wessex pharaoh of the pyramid of Cheops. Three brutal intrusions into its interior, one in 1776, one in 1849, and one watched by television cameras over the period 1968–70, found nothing to prove that its purpose was as a burial mound. The last excavations found plant remains at the core of the mound which gave a radio-carbon dating of 2600 BC. Michael Dames in his study *The Silbury Treasure*,

42 *Above* West Kennet, Wiltshire. The entrance to the long barrow seen behind the giant sarsen stones that may symbolize ox horns.

43 *Right* Avebury, Wiltshire. Giant sarsens in the south-western circle.

after studying the setting of the mound, not only in relation to the deliberately planned lake and ring walls about it but also to features of the surrounding landscape, especially the rising nearby at the Swallowhead of the river Kennet, has come to the conclusion that 'Silbury is the Great Goddess, pregnant'.[6] Her womb is the mound formed almost wholly from the quarry about it which was then filled with the water that delineated the rest of her body. Her body together with the mound appears in the squatting position giving birth familiar in numerous examples of figures of the Neolithic Great Goddess. Michael Dames has also demonstrated that Silbury is aligned with solstitial and equinoctial events and suggests that its most important seasonal rite would have been at harvest-time or Lammastide. It is a harvest hill and in its closeness to the henge and stone circles of Avebury it shares a feature now noted in several other sites of the period—the combination of a harvest hill with a henge as at Arbor Low in Derbyshire and Knowlton in Dorset.

Avebury, which has not been dated by radio-carbon means, is nevertheless thought to be coeval with Silbury. It is the greatest of the 900 henge or stone circle monuments that either survive or are known to have existed in Great Britain. Its immense earthworks enclose an area of 28 acres with a bank now varying in height but which from depth of inner ditch to top was 51 ft. Within this encircling bank and ditch stood an outer circle of about a hundred sarsen stones, which remain only in part. There were two inner circles, the northern and southern inner circles within the outer circumference. At the centre of the south circle stood a 21-ft-high stone called by William Stukeley in the eighteenth century the 'Obelisk' and since destroyed. It was part of an inner pattern of sarsens known by its shape as the D feature. Also according to Stukeley two avenues of sarsens led the main approaches to Avebury, one the Beckhampton avenue, almost wholly lost, and the other the West Kennet avenue of which much survives in original or restored form. The whole ensemble according to Stukeley's engraving (pl. 45) formed a serpentine form leading into and away from the immense belly of Avebury itself. The West Kennet avenue, whose pattern of thin stones facing fat stones can be interpreted as alternations of the Goddess as virgin and pregnant woman, leads to the Sanctuary on Overton Hill—a site largely destroyed in the eighteenth century but with the positions of its stones and the postholes for its timber building now clearly marked. The sarsens of Avebury, sandstone boulders of immense size, were brought from the Marlborough downs. An unhappy ritual under the auspices of the Church in the Middle Ages decreed the destruction of a stone once every twenty-five years: they were cracked by fire and broken up. The body of a fourteenth-century barber-surgeon was found crushed by a stone he was attempting to topple. The rate of destruction increased in the eighteenth century, even while Stukeley was studying the monument, when a local farmer, 'Stonekiller' Robinson, with benighted purpose led gangs of men to burn and smash the stones. Despite their hard work, enough remains of Avebury to make it one of the most impressive sites in the country. It is large enough to hold part of the village of Avebury within its enclosure and yet give a full idea of its vastness and ancient spirit. It possesses to an exceptional degree the one quality of the ancient sites of this period that is beyond the arguments of archaeologists about its purpose: it is very beautiful, being full of subtle features rising into sight and sinking into invisibility with the weather and the time of day and arousing in the visitor that state of waking dreaming through which the contrasts of ancient stone and young grass, the shadows in the lines of solifluction on the heaped

44 Avebury. Sarsens of the Kennet avenue which in its original complete form led from the Sanctuary at Overton to Avebury and may have formed a processional way for the women at the spring festivities of the Great Goddess. The Beckhampton avenue may have provided a similar route for the men coming from the other direction.

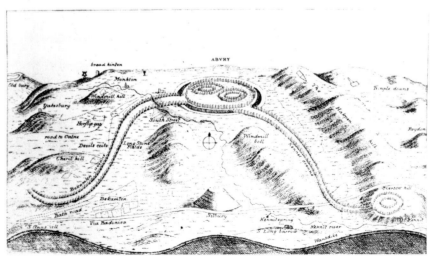

45 Avebury. An engraving from William Stukeley's *Abury Described* (1743), showing the two avenues, the Beckhampton avenue (*left*) and the Kennet avenue (*right*) leading to the henge at Avebury. Almost nothing remains of the Beckhampton avenue.

banks, and the sense of a living landscape, combine to enhance the pleasures of looking and of simply being there. Avebury is big enough to take large numbers of visitors and to dominate them with its mood so that, whatever their attitude or behaviour when they arrive, they are quietened by it.

Immense as it is, the meaning and quality of Avebury is best appreciated when it is seen as part of the whole surrounding complex of monuments. If West Kennet Long Barrow is the Goddess as hag, and Silbury is the harvest Goddess giving birth, then Avebury is the bridal Goddess, the place of conception. The dual sexual imagery of the snake, of the snake as phallus and of the snake with its open mouth as vulva, is combined in the symbolism of the henge where the line of the Beckhampton avenue, that of the males, meets in the south circle the avenue of the women coming from Overton sanctuary. As one travels from site to site in this region so one gets a fuller and fuller feeling for their relationships and significance, from the view of Silbury and West Kennet from the sanctuary, for example, or the mysterious long shape of Waden Hill when one stands in the avenue by the stone pointing to the midsummer sunrise. All these sites were probably specially venerated at different times of the year according to the seasonal moods of the Goddess; all of them show aspects of her and may be contained within an even bigger depiction of her delineated by a series of camps and barrows covering several square miles.

If Avebury is big enough to absorb visiting crowds, this, alas, is not the case with the far more famous Stonehenge which is being worn away by its visitors. It is a very complicated site, both in the various stages of its construction and in the astronomical functions it may have served. Since it received one of its first literary mentions, by Geoffrey of Monmouth in the twelfth century, Stonehenge has been getting older and older. Geoffrey ascribed its construction to Merlin who brought the stones to Wiltshire from Mount Killaraus in Ireland, to satisfy the demands of Ambrosius Aurelius, uncle of King Arthur, for a memorial fit for the British noblemen treacherously murdered by the Saxons.[7] This would put its date in the fifth century AD. Inigo Jones, visiting it from Wilton in the company of James I, declared it to be the work of the Romans. A contemporary of his said it was built by the Danes. It was put further back in time by John Aubrey and then in the next century William Stukeley pronounced it to be anterior to the Romans and the work of the Celtic druids. By the beginning of the twentieth century it was thought to be even earlier—the construction of megalith builders present in this country a thousand years before the successive Celtic invasions from Europe. As it was pushed back further and further into the past so it appeared that less and less could be said of its purpose and the nature of its builders. The application of radio-carbon dating put its main stages of construction at between 2000 and 1600 BC; then, when the discovery of a basic error in the system of radio-carbon dating led to a major revision of the chronology of this period, Stonehenge once more went further back in time to between 2800 BC and 2000–1800 BC. The dates have now stuck, for the time being, at this point and the stages of construction are generally agreed to break down into three. The first, Stonehenge I made about 2800 BC, consisted of the digging of the circular ditch forming a bank broken by a causeway facing the Heelstone. To this period are assigned the mysterious Aubrey Holes (named after their discoverer John Aubrey) which may have held marker posts for observing the cycle of lunar eclipses. In about 2400 BC Stonehenge II came into being at the beginning of the Bronze Age, probably the work of the new race known from their pottery as the Beaker folk. They realigned the monument so that its major

46 Stonehenge. A view between two trilithons showing bluestones and, beyond, part of the lintelled outer ring of sarsens.

astronomical alignment was to the midsummer sunrise. They may also have erected the four Station Stones which form a precise rectangle across the centre of the henge. Most astonishing of their achievements was to bring 82 bluestones from the Prescelly Mountains in south-west Wales in order to erect them as a double circle in the centre of the monument. Geoffrey of Monmouth's story about Merlin may be a folk memory of this achievement. The third phase of construction is divided into three, IIIa, IIIb, and IIIc. For Stonehenge IIIa, in about 2100 BC, the great sarsens on Marlborough down twenty miles away were shaped and hauled across the country to be erected into the five trilithons, standing in a horseshoe in the centre, and the ring of lintelled stones encircling the horseshoe. To carry out this work the ring of bluestones had been taken down and carefully preserved. In the remaining phases, IIIb and IIIc, the bluestones were brought back and arranged first in one order and then in their present and final state in about 1600 BC. The work of Professor A. Thom and his family in surveying Stonehenge has served not only to confirm the opinions of many earlier students that it had great astronomical significance but also to make it appear as the central point of a solar and lunar observatory with foresights on surrounding hillsides or man-made prominences.

I cannot help feeling that the use of Stonehenge as an observatory was only one of its purposes, an ancillary and related purpose certainly. It was and is a place of power and a great work of art, capable of drawing the respect of and inspiring the succeeding generations who worked on it, not only to emulate, but to surpass, their fathers and predecessors over a period of 1,200 years. The nearby henge sites of Durrington Walls and Woodhenge, with their immense wooden circular houses, may have been the dwelling or gathering places of the priestly astronomers presumed to have been responsible for the design and erection of Stonehenge. What we lack for our understanding of it is the knowledge of the dominating symbol or group of symbols which gave its inspiration, though Michael Dames has suggested an interpretation of it as an architectural expression of the same ideas earlier expressed in the earthworks of Silbury and Avebury.[8]

Turning to the far north there is on the Mainland of Orkney an associated series of monuments remarkably comparable to both the Silbury–Avebury–Overton complex and the Stonehenge–Durrington Walls–Woodhenge complex in Wiltshire. This consists of the great chambered tomb of Maeshowe, with, close by, the Stones of Stenness connected by an avenue leading to the Ring of Brodgar. A few miles off is the Neolithic village of Skara Brae which has been described as fulfilling the same function for these Orkney monuments as Overton sanctuary did for Avebury, namely being the gathering or living place of the astronomer-priests. Of these sites all are fascinating but Maeshowe bears the crown because not only is it the finest chambered tomb in north-west Europe but one of the greatest works of architecture in these islands. All you see from the outside is a mound about 25 ft high. Taken into it by the guide, you have to stoop along a passage only slightly more than 4 ft high and extending for 31 ft. The walls and roof of this passage are built of stone slabs some 18 ft long. Once through this passage you stand upright in a chamber 15 ft square with three cells off the main chamber. The immense slabs, layer on layer of them, some so finely joined that a knife cannot slip between them, are piled high in straight walls that then start to corbel out to make a pyramidal ceiling. The Vikings, who in the twelfth century broke into Maeshowe to look for treasure and left rune marks and other carvings, broke the summit of the ceiling and further damage

47 *Left, above* Prescelly mountains, Dyfed. These mountains were the source of the 82 bluestones that were transported probably by sea and river to Salisbury Plain for the second stage of construction of Stonehenge.

48 *Left, below* Wood-henge, Wiltshire. Markers of the sites of the postholes that, when excavated, provided evidence of a vast wooden edifice not far from Stonehenge. This and the nearby Durrington Walls may have been the living-quarters of the priesthood associated with Stonehenge.

was done by an excavation in 1861 so that the chamber is now sealed from the weather by a modern domed roof. The corbelled stones are supported by piers faced with monoliths that give a powerful counter-effect of verticality to the horizontal rhythm of the wall and ceiling slabs. The function of Maeshowe is said to be solely funerary. I find it hard to believe that a construction so dramatic in the contrast achieved between the passage and the chamber, so skilfully and beautifully made, so clearly intended to be looked at and admired, should have been an infrequently disturbed mausoleum and not also a place of ritual and initiation. Few architectural effects, in my experience, are more memorable than the impression of the wall and corbelled sheets of stone extending out like long chords of music chanted by many voices.

Only a short distance away stand the henge sites of the Stones of Stenness and the Ring of Brodgar linked by an avenue on the isthmus between the Lochs of Stenness and of Harray. Though Stenness has the larger stones, only four of them are still standing and the Ring of Brodgar with 27 of its 60-odd stones still erect is the more powerful and impressive monument. The lichenous stones rise out of the heather and, seen against the waters of the loch, make a magical and peaceful sight. Brodgar has been proved to have significant astronomical alignments and perhaps the builders and guardians of these shrines lived five miles away on the coast in the extraordinary Stone Age village of Skara Brae. Built on the dunes of a beach where the seals poke their heads out of the sea demanding to be sung and danced to, this village was overwhelmed in a sandstorm nearly 3,000 years ago. Its discovery and excavation revealed a cluster of ten houses with furniture built of stone slabs, and with deep middens whose siftings revealed information of endless fascination about the lives of its inhabitants. What is important in the present context is that the shape of the houses seems to represent the image of the Great Mother, in a manner similar to earlier dwellings also associated with temples on the Maltese island of Gozo. This would mean that the inhabitants actually lived within their matrix deity.

The people of Skara Brae used the same pottery known as grooved ware which is associated with other ritual sites throughout Great Britain and Ireland. Engraved often with the spiral and chevron pattern that characterizes the great stones of New Grange, this pottery came from a place with specialized potteries that has not been identified. This and other features that these scattered communities have in common such as a reverence for ritual stone axes or the possession of a common unit of measurement (the megalithic yard) are amongst the evidence for a special priestly caste capable of handing down knowledge from one generation to another and in communication with one another for the purposes of trade and the practice of their religion.[9] Of course, this picture of an élite supported by the labours of a docile population of farmers may be merely the projection of donnish minds back to a golden age when professors ruled and taught and were obeyed. It may not have been like that at all. Interpreted another way, the evidence allows us to think of it as a matriarchal society held together by a deep and homogeneous myth that was made true with every action of the cycle of the farming year, a society in which poetry, art, and the dance were necessary to the sprouting of the crops and the increase of cattle and one in which the people shared equally in the pleasures of life and its labours. This could equally well be criticized as the phantasy world of poets and symbol-loving psychiatrists longing for a society whose words are as alive as animals in an environment that reflects the archetypes of the soul.

There is a division between the two ways of interpreting this distant society

49 Skara Brae, Orkney. The seaside village of stone houses whose shapes may be deliberate evocations of the Great Goddess. These houses may have been the living-quarters of the priesthood associated with Maeshowe, the Ring of Brodgar, and the Stones of Stenness.

which may be resolved in this way. Matriarchal societies are conservative, slow to change, egalitarian, moon-dominated, moon-weighted. As the ice-caps retreated after the last Ice Age, man could have remained as a wandering hunter, his numbers few, his possibilities of higher development limited. If those possibilities were to develop, he had to learn to stay in one place, to settle down and win his food from the earth, no longer from the forest. If for hundreds of generations he had lived on the move, everything in his inherited and social instincts would have fought against the unnaturalness of settling down to a life of farming. What more powerful way of enforcing him to settle could be devised than a religion centred on Earth herself, the Great Goddess, a religion whose tenets dictated the cycle of labour in the year and the forms of society, whose symbolism inspired the interpretation of all natural phenomena from the

50 *Left* Beaghmore, Tyrone. Stone circles, cairns, and alignments: an important site revealed by peat cutting, this is said to be Neolithic and Bronze Age in date.

51 *Below left* Shovel Down, Devon. A processional way or avenue of standing stones on Dartmoor, Bronze Age in date and associated with cairns and a burial chamber.

52 *Below right* Lough Gur, Limerick. A view of the Lios, the largest of surviving Irish stone circles with a diameter of 150 ft backed by an earthen bank. There are many other monuments, stone circles and burial chambers around the banks of Lough Gur.

53 Drombeg, West Cork. A recumbent stone circle on a terrace looking out to sea: a view showing the flat altar stone. The portal stones are aligned on the setting sun at the winter solstice.

growing of grass to the movement of heavenly bodies? Such a religion could impose a unity upon society that would work ever more strongly over succeeding generations to eradicate the ancient and ingrained nomadic desire. How, though, could such a society escape the traps of settled society, the inertia, the rigidity and conservatism of farming communities which could limit the development of man's higher possibilities as effectively as though he had never cut down the primeval forest which was his illimitable environment as a hunter? How better than by engaging on works by the thousand all over the inhabited parts of these islands—not just the greater sites such as Silbury or Avebury—which would require planning and direction by men and women with specialized knowledge, transmitting and increasing that knowledge from one generation to another and creating a tradition of change that would inspire the children to emulate and surpass their parents? It would fit better with the matriarchal nature of society if we thought of the leaders of the great building campaigns not as astronomer-priests but as astronomer-priestesses, as wise women, the noble ancestresses of the medieval and later witches who, devoted to the degenerated scraps of belief and lore they had inherited, died at the stake for their inheritance.

54 *Overleaf* Callanish, Isle of Lewis. A Circle of 13 stones approached by avenues. A single stone stands in the centre of the circle close to a cairn. Callanish, which is sometimes dated to about 1800 BC, stands on a promontory beside Loch Roag.

To make these great monuments, digging out the ditches with picks of the antlers the red deer shed seasonally in the forests and removing the earth or chalk with ox blades, they certainly laboured. Silbury, it has been calculated, would have taken 500 men, working continuously, fifteen years to build. What they were undoubtedly helped by was an excellent climate providing cloudless night skies that enabled reliable and constant observation of the heavens and warm temperate weather that favoured their crops. It was probably the

worsening of the weather from about 1500 BC together with disease and the exhaustion of the land that brought about a rapid decline in their civilization. Within the period from about 4000 BC to that sudden ending—a period longer than that from the beginning of our era to the present day—we can look back to a remarkable sequence of achievements: the introduction of farming, both arable and pastoral, the domestication of animals and the clearing of land, the introduction of architecture in the early stone monuments, and following that, the creation of some of the most complex buildings and earthworks based in their design on a common measure and a knowledge of the heavens, with, in addition, the remarkable fusion between the races of the late Neolithic culture and the new men of the Bronze Age which brought about continuity of use in the religious and ritual sites and traditions. Thus there is a link in Ireland between the stone circle set about New Grange in 3300 BC and the late stone circle of Drombeg in West Cork or between the Stonehenge of the North, Callanish, dated to about 1800 BC, and the numerous smaller stone circles built over a long period in many parts of Scotland. That continuity lasted in many cases during the Iron Age and even into the Christian era. The Dorset henge of Knowlton has a twelfth-century church built in its centre and there are many other examples of churches which include megaliths either in their structures or in their graveyards and surroundings.

Up to this century many of the megalithic sites have been used continuously for ceremonies that derived from Neolithic rituals; till the 1930s a maypole was erected close to the destroyed obelisk stone at Avebury. At Callendar in Scotland up to the end of the eighteenth century a ritual game with a simulated sacrifice of one of the players took place in an earthen henge dug anew each year. The belief that the stones are living creatures is widespread; the Rollright stones are said on certain nights to rush down the hill to drink from the nearby river. Other stones are said to dance or like the Merry Maidens in Cornwall to have been girls turned to stone for dancing on a Sunday. The most notable example of the barely coherent spiritual urges that these ancient sites inspire is given by Stonehenge.

On the subject of Stonehenge our imaginations are trained by visions such as this of Wordsworth's in *The Prelude*, drawing on the time when he wandered on Salisbury Plain:

> gently was I charmed
> Into a waking dream, a reverie
> That, with believing eyes, where'er I turned
> Beheld long-bearded teachers, with white wands
> Uplifted, pointing to the starry sky,
> Alternately, and plain below, while breath
> Of music swayed their motions, and the waste
> Rejoiced with them and me in those sweet sounds.[10]

And some people such as the modern organizations of druids take the trouble to give the vision form and life, as may be seen at Stonehenge on the night and dawn of the Summer Solstice.

Stonehenge at this time of the year has become a meeting-place not only for the druids but for great numbers of people inspired by the alternative culture that grew up in the nineteen-sixties—not to mention the television crews, the photographers and the Wiltshire constabulary with their Alsatians. Many go there because they believe it is one of the great power centres of these islands: some think this great nexus of power is in the earth below the stones. Others regard it as the navel of an invisible cord binding this planet to intergalactic wombs of knowledge and as the device on to which visitors from other worlds have homed in other ages. They come with their minds fed with the sober theories of Professor Thom, with the hypothesis of the leys of Alfred Watkins, and with a host of other ideas and conjectures.

Clive Hicks and I were among the fortunate allowed into the stones themselves on this night: fortunate because the crowds gathering there are now so great that the police hold them behind a wide circle of barbed wire temporarily erected for the night. There with the photographers, the journalists, the policemen, and the lady with a loud voice who had come to make a protest, we waited among the stones while the wind that had driven the rain away brought delicious draughts of scent from the flowers and the trodden grass of the plain and the downs. Then, while it was still night, announced by cheers and catcalls from the crowd of about two thousand watchers hemming the perimeter of barbed wire, the druids appeared. About forty figures dressed in white moved in line towards the stones but did not enter them. Quietly, at the four quarters of Stonehenge, they placed symbols of the four elements, leaving at each station three druids to guard them while the rest withdrew. Each group of three stood still and silent while the noise from the crowd grew and subsided.

With the lightening of the sky the stones were revealed in grey, with their bearded and mottled lichens standing out like a myriad eyebrows and eyes. After about an hour the main body of druids returned, went to each trio of their companions they had left on guard, gathered them to themselves and went down to the Heelstone, the sarsen that marks the rising of the sun on this particular morning of the year. Unperturbed by the photographers dancing about them and the often hostile and constant hubbub of the crowd, they conducted their rites with grace and composure. The time for sunrise grew near and the cloud on the horizon seemed too thick for us to hope that the sun would be visible. I overheard a policeman saying, 'This is my twentieth Stonehenge and I've only seen it rise three or four times. It won't happen today. Now, last year it was beautiful. You should've seen it last year. It won't happen today.' The druids returned from the Heelstone and formed a circle inside the stones. Everyone was looking towards the eastern sky, which was streaked with long thin grey clouds like branches touched with a lively pink like clusters of peach blossom. Then suddenly there it was: a red-gold fruit, the sun of our dreams made real above the Heelstone; and a cheer went up from the crowd; the chief druid muttered prayers; the cockney lady made her protest; the photographers jostled one another and us; and all theories, all prejudices, all useless thoughts fled like night before this gift of a moment that signified that Earth, having reached one of the two furthest points of her annual and elliptical journey, was bowing her northern hemisphere in deepest obeisance to the Sun.

The ceremonies continued. The faces of the druids, male and female, had in many cases the unconscious beauty that only comes from the stirring of deepest emotions. Then they filed away and with them most of the crowd and the photographers. The cockney lady explained her case to some sympathetic listeners. The rain came back and of the vast numbers held back by the barbed wire only two in wide hats remained singing a wild, sad, and repetitive tune to which one of them strummed a guitar underneath his cloak.

Chapter 3

Poets, groves, and kings: Celtic and Iron Age sites

The noblest qualities of the heroes of the ancient Celts are recorded in the extraordinary debate[1] between St Patrick and the last of their number, Oisin, who returns from the Land of the Young to find a different Ireland, one where, in the place of battles, he sees 'the crozier of Patrick being carried; and his clerks at their quarrelling'. He maintains to Patrick the virtues he and his companions followed throughout their lives: 'truth that was in our hearts, and strength in our arms, and fulfilment in our tongues'. In praising Finn he speaks of his generosity, that ultimate test of the leader of a warrior aristocracy: 'If the brown leaves falling in the woods were gold, if the white waves were silver, Finn would have given away the whole of it.'

With such attitudes we come to a different world from that of the megalith builders. An old triad speaks of three things that are holy: poets, groves, and kings. The appearance of kings in this grouping signifies the new masculine domination in society that is a feature of the Iron Age invaders and also of the increasingly warlike nature of the times that required the leadership of warriors. The balance between the sexes that would appear to have been a characteristic of the matriarchal society of the Neolithic and Bronze Age periods was upset, with consequences that are still to be put right today. The poets and the groves refer to the members and holy places of the druids.

One of Julius Caesar's reasons for his invasion of Britain in 44–3 BC was to stamp out the centre of druidic culture to which the Gauls looked across the channel for their education and the continued inspiration for their resistance. The religion and the culture of the druids is now thought to be of immemorial antiquity, keeping a continuity with the Neolithic and Bronze Age beliefs and sites, as was shown by excavations at Cairnpapple Hill, West Lothian, which includes a Neolithic henge, a Bronze Age stone circle and burials with a burial ground of Iron Age date. This continuity is all the more remarkable because of the series of invasions which brought the first Iron Age peoples and later the Celts to Britain and Ireland. Ancient Irish traditions speak of a series of invasions, of the great race of the Tuatha de Danaan who overcame the indigenous inhabitants, the Firbolg. They in turn were displaced by the Milesians, the sons of the Gael. Though it is difficult to relate the Irish invasions with the archaeological record, these stories may well reflect the series of upheavals and migrations that affected Europe and the Middle East from 1200 BC with the fall of the Hittite Empire and the release of their close-guarded secrets of ironworking to other races. The earliest known Celtic society, called the Hallstatt culture after the Austrian village where it was first discovered, predates 1000 BC. It reached the coasts of Britain from the seventh century BC onwards, bringing a new aggressive tone into the static and generally peaceful nature of Bronze Age life. The great explosion of Celtic energy derives from the culture known as La Tène, centred on the valleys of the Rhône and the Marne. These Celts are the first to attract the notice of classical historians, and with good reason; their raids and conquests stretched far eastwards into Greece and present-day Turkey and southwards into Italy, culminating in the sack of Rome in 387 BC. The La Tène Celts also came across the Channel and by 100 BC had established themselves in all parts of the British Isles. The last invasion before the Roman conquests was that of the Belgae, who settled a wide area north and south of the Thames valley with their chief centres at Silchester, St Albans, and Colchester.

The characteristic constructions of the Iron Age were the hillforts, huge

55 South Cadbury, Somerset. A view showing a rampart of the Iron Age hillfort, a site containing a Celtic temple with ritual pits. Traditionally the site of Arthur's Camelot, South Cadbury was refortified in late Roman times and at the start of the Dark Ages.

defensive enclosures befitting the warlike nature of the new society. Some of these include what have been described as temple sites. Maiden Castle, the tribal centre of the Durotriges, the most spectacular hillfort of all, which was stormed by Vespasian in his conquest of the south-west, contained a circular temple on the site of which in the late Romano–British period another temple was built. At South Cadbury, which we will meet again as the most likely candidate for King Arthur's Camelot, the Iron Age hillfort contained the traces of a rectangular temple approached through a series of ritual pits with animals buried in them. On the site of Heathrow airport a similar rectangular temple dating from about 400 BC was found. Probably all hillforts fulfilled a ritual as well as an administrative and a defensive function since they were the centres of the tribes which made up Celtic society. Many of them retain a powerful and mysterious atmosphere such as the camp on the Sinodun Hills at Dorchester-on-Thames. The one that best shows the combination of elements that went to make up a tribal centre is the hillfort at Uffington on the Berkshire downs, set close to a stretch of the far more ancient track known as the Ridgeway. On the slope of a natural amphitheatre in the downs close to the hillfort is the earliest known chalk cut figure in England, the White Horse of Uffington, sacred, it is thought, to the Celtic horse goddess Epona. Below it is the artificially flattened mound called Dragon's Hill, where according to legend St George killed the dragon. The bare patches where no grass grows mark where the dragon's blood was spilt. Some, indeed, think that the White Horse, which resembles a design on coins of the first century BC, may be a recutting of a dragon figure.[2]

The savage and warlike nature of the Celts is manifested in certain aspects of their religious practices both as reported by classical writers and as archaeologists have revealed. Caesar and other writers give terrifying descriptions of mass immolations of human victims burnt inside wickerwork images. A particular power in Celtic legends attaches to severed heads and their association with sacred wells and places. In the *Mabinogion* the severed head of Bran the Blessed converses pleasantly for 89 years and then on its instructions is buried on the site of the Tower of London to guard Britain from invasion. Sinister shrines furnished with skulls have been found in Wookey Hole and many sacred springs have given up skulls, amongst other offerings. The practice of displaying the skulls of enemies and traitors over city gates and on London Bridge (again a water association) may date back to the early Celtic period.

This particular cult may be the product of a degenerative stage in the long history of the druids, just as the phenomenal hunger of the Aztecs for human sacrifice would seem to be a marked degeneration of the Mayan culture they conquered and superseded. This would help to account for the paradoxical nature of Celtic society which at the same time could be so aggressively barbarous and yet produce works of art and a body of living myth of lasting power and effect.

Celtic society was threefold, divided into the druids (priests, poets and prophets), the warriors, and the farming peasantry. Julius Caesar said the druids were under the rule of an arch-druid and that they officiated at the worship of the gods, ruled on religious questions, educated the young, and judged disputes. He particularly stressed their belief in immortality: 'A lesson they take particular pains to inculcate is that the soul does not perish, but after death passes from one body to another; they think this the best incentive to bravery because it teaches men to disregard the terrors of death.'[3] He also speaks of the range of their cosmological studies and reflections and of their belief in one supreme god, Dis Pater.

Many scholars in recent years, especially the brothers Rees, have brought out the numerous resemblances between Sanskrit practices and myths and those of the Celts. One of the most interesting parallels comes from the dual religious and druidic centres of Ireland, Tara, the seat of the High King, and Uisnech. 'It would appear', say the brothers Rees, 'that Tara originally symbolized the cosmos of the gods as opposed to the chaos of the demons, Uisnech as the primeval unity, the principle in which all oppositions are resolved.' This duality they compare to dual ritual sites in India and in Rome.[4]

Tara is an example of a conceptual idea that could be imposed on any territory once it was conquered or organized. It is the fifth direction of space, that of 'here' surrounded by the four provinces of Ulster, Munster, Connacht and Leinster,

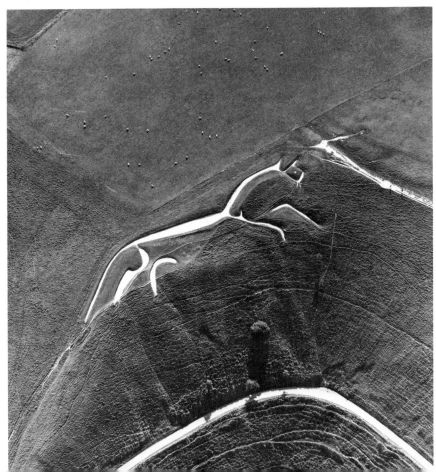

56 *Above* Sinodun Hills, Oxfordshire. The Iron Age hillfort now covered by beech-trees, known as Wittenham Clumps. It is sited close to the Thames and the later town of Dorchester on Thames which was the centre of the mission of St Birinus.

57 *Right* Uffington, Oxfordshire. An aerial view of the White Horse of Uffington. The Iron Age hillfort is on the right. Out of the photograph, to the left, is the Dragon's Hill.

58 *Above* Tara, Meath. The Stone of Destiny with a view of the Mound of the Hostages, a passage grave dating from *c.* 1800 BC. The remains of the banqueting hall lie on the slope of the hill to the left. The trees partly mask a church.

59 *Left* Turoe, Galway. The Stone of Turoe, a navel stone with its top covered with curvilinear ornament associated with the La Tène culture. It was removed from the Rath of Feerwore, dated to the late pagan Celtic era, to its present site.

60 River Darent, Kent. 'The poets thought it was always on the brink of water poetry was revealed to them.' This particular river features in the paintings of the visionary artist Samuel Palmer, when he lived at Shoreham.

north, south, west and east. Still on the summit of Tara stands a stone called the Lìs Fal or Stone of Destiny which shrieked with a loud voice when touched by the chariot wheels of a man chosen to be king. This stone, which is also simply characterized as 'the stone penis', showing that the king must be recognized by the embodiment of the male principle, may be the original or it may have been set by the Irish rebels in 1798 who conducted a desperate stand against the English at Tara. At Uisnech there was a central stone known as the stone of divisions and called the navel of Ireland. Such a navel stone is the remarkably carved Stone of Turoe in Connemara, like a stubby puff-ball incised with swirling ornament. A similar division of the land appears in Wales which survived into the creation of the four bishoprics of Bangor, St Asaph, Llandaff, and St Davids, all meeting at the point of the five-peaked mountain Pumlumon. [5]

The fascination with boundaries, with the places of the meeting of unlike such as river and riverbank, with sites such as Tara or Uisnech that appeared to offer points of entry from mysterious otherworlds, are characteristic of Celtic thought and mythology. Finn Mac Cumhal, the great Irish hero, went to study poetry with a poet who lived by the Boyne, 'for the poets thought it was always on the brink of water poetry was revealed to them', [6] and there by catching and cooking one of the salmon of knowledge he gained insight and wisdom. The reverence for rivers felt by the Celts was so great that they would have the most elaborate offerings made, such as the famous shield now in the British Museum, solely for the purpose of throwing them into the water. This shield was thrown into the Thames at Battersea. The site of Llyn Cerrig Bach in Anglesey has revealed an astonishing number of artefacts offered in this way. It is significant that many rivers in England retain their Celtic names; such was the power attaching to them that the Anglo-Saxons could not supersede them with appellations of their own. One has only to go to a great river such as the Thames, the Severn, the Boyne or the Shannon and watch the eddies making their spiral patterns like the triskele forms on Celtic bronzework to experience the mood and atmosphere that these forebears of ours especially felt there.

The other great centres of holiness for the druids were their groves and clearings in forests. Many of the classical authors, writing of the druids, refer to the awe in which such places were held. Meanings and symbolic associations attached to all trees, most especially to the oak. When the oak bore mistletoe (something almost unheard of nowadays), the druids would cut the mistletoe down with golden sickles, after which two white bulls would be sacrificed. The most important centre of these groves was across the Menai Strait on Anglesey. It was to destroy this nest of druid power that the Roman general Suetonius Paulinus in AD 61 conducted a swift and brilliant campaign across Wales.

His attack across the Menai Strait was completely successful. Tacitus describes the scene:

The enemy lined the shore in a dense armed mass. Among them were black-robed women with dishevelled hair like Furies, brandishing torches. Close by stood Druids, raising their hands to heaven and screaming dreadful curses. This weird spectacle awed the Roman soldiers into a sort of paralysis. They stood still—and presented themselves as a target. But then they urged each other (and were urged by the general) not to fear a horde of fanatical women. Onward pressed their standards and they bore down their opponents, enveloping them in the flames of their own torches.[7]

The groves were cut down, the curses of the druids were of no avail and though their religion was to survive, their political power was destroyed.

Chapter 4

The ideal of the city: Roman religion and early Christianity

When the Emperor Claudius led in person the campaign that successfully began the Roman conquest of Britain in AD 43, he seized the capital of his chief opponents, the Trinovantes, at Camulodunum (now Colchester), the fortress of the wargod Camulus, and created there a legionary fortress. In AD 49–50 it became a colonia or town settled by ex-soldiers on conquered territory and the authorities built there among other official buildings a vast classical temple dedicated to the Emperor Claudius. Tacitus described it as the 'stronghold of everlasting domination'[1]; its size and splendour brought remark even at Rome and its presence as the centre of the Roman state religion centred on the *numen* or divine spirit of the Emperor was one of the many resentments that caused the rebellion led by Boudicca, queen of the Iceni, in AD 60. Tacitus describes the portents before her descent on Colchester. The statue of Victory fell down, her

61 Colchester, Essex. A model of the Temple of Claudius: the 'stronghold of everlasting domination', built to commemorate the Emperor Claudius' conquest in AD 43 and probably the chief centre of the Roman state religion in Britain up to about AD 350, by which time Christianity had become the official imperial religion.

62 Brading, Isle of Wight. One of a series of fourth-century mosaics in the Roman villa: this depicts a cockerel-headed god from one of the Roman mystery religions, possibly Abraxes. The ladder may symbolize the soul's ascent to heaven.

back turned as though in retreat from the enemy. Women in frenzy chanted of approaching destruction and said the cries of the barbarian had been heard in the council chamber, that the theatre had re-echoed with shrieks, that a reflection of the colonia overthrown had been seen in the estuary of the Thames. The sea appeared blood-red, and spectres of human corpses were left behind as the tide receded.[2] Boudicca's forces besieged the soldiers in the temple for two days and slaughtered the inhabitants. She then continued to the destruction of Verulamium (St Albans) and London before her rebellion was savagely crushed and she committed suicide.

The temple was restored and important Britons were required to serve on a yearly basis as its priests, paying for the rites and sacrifices associated with the imperial cult. A model of it (pl. 61) stands in the Museum in the Norman keep of the castle built by William the Conqueror on part of the podium of the temple. A great flight of steps led up the podium to the portico of the temple with six or eight columns supporting the pediment. In front of the temple stood the altar flanked by statues within an impressive courtyard surrounding the precinct, which covered five acres. The temple probably remained the chief centre of the state religion of Rome in the province of Britain up to AD 350.

The importation of this state religion was a most important event in the religious and social consciousness of the inhabitants of these islands—as important as the transition to agriculture in the Neolithic period—for two reasons. One was that the religion was deliberately supranational, including all the tribes and nations within the Roman Empire from Parthia to the lands of the Picts beyond the Roman Walls of North Britain. The other was that it introduced the idea of the city into these islands as the regional reflection of the great city of

Rome so that every township with its forum and temples became the centre of religious and administrative activity and the focus of civilization. The change of emphasis remains in the very words 'civilization' and 'paganism', 'civilization' being the culture of the *civitas* or city and paganism the superstitious and narrow beliefs of the *pagus* or countryside. The chief gods of the Roman state religion were the Capitoline deities of Jupiter, Juno, and Minerva and these were often associated with the cult of the Emperor and his dead deified predecessors. The worship of these and other gods and goddesses of the Mediterranean world was brought to Britain and soon spread amongst the native population, with interesting assimilations to local cults. These customs and beliefs originating in Etruscan and early Roman townships had become the basis of the state religion largely through the efforts of the Emperor Augustus to found a cult that would assist in the stabilizing of society after the long disturbances of the civil wars and that would enhance imperial authority with the glamour of divinity. Remains from Romano–British towns reveal how many households possessed shrines adorned with a model temple as a home for the *lares* (the gods of the family or ancestors) and the *penates* (the gods of the larder) and with statues of particularly favoured deities. The founding of towns would have been accompanied by rites the Romans had absorbed from the Etruscans, the invocation of the gods for choice of a favourable site, the consultation of omens, the marking out by plough of the perimeter where the walls were to stand, and the special rite associated with the naming of the town.[3] Similar rites attended the founding of temples and shrines. The walls of a town were considered especially sacred.

Most Romano–British towns have survived or been resettled so successfully

63 Silchester, Hampshire. An aerial view showing the irregular line of the walls with grid patterns of the streets. The amphitheatre is outside the walls, covered in trees (*bottom right*). The twelfth-century church built on the site of one of the town's Romano-British temples stands within the walls (*lower centre right*).

that it is difficult to recapture their special and sacred nature. Silchester is one of the few that never regained its status after the Dark Ages. Silchester was the tribal centre of the Atrobates and the Romans called it Calleva Atrebatum. Although there have been several excavations there and many important discoveries, both of buildings and of artefacts, have been made on the site, nothing remains above ground except long expanses of the walls and an amphitheatre outside the town. The stone facing has long been ripped away from the walls so what one walks beside is a long high rugged cliff of large flints embedded in mortar, strengthened with courses of flat sandstones. The isolation of the place, in the north Hampshire countryside, and the lack of any buildings except a farm and an old church built on or close to the site of one of the Romano–British temples at the edge of the walls concentrate the mind upon the

64 Bath, Avon. The Great Bath sacred to the Celtic goddess Sul-Minerva and once associated with a temple dedicated to her. This bath originally had a vaulted roof. The colonnade is nineteenth-century.

significance of the changes brought about by the Roman invasion. The desire to live together in an urban group was something that arose far away in the Levant and the Mediterranean when men founded their religious and social impulses not on the tribe but on the *polis*, the city which was itself a god. The excellent aerial photographs in the small museum of Silchester show clearly, together with other reconstructions, the grid system first devised by Etruscan augurs on which the town was laid out. The typical Romano–British temples suggest a fusion of Celtic and Roman beliefs. Also beneath the soil lie the remains of an early Christian church—said to be the earliest known Christian church north of the Alps. Silchester also appears in Arthurian legend as the town where King Arthur was crowned, according to Geoffrey of Monmouth.[4] As if to emphasize the continuity of religious practice and the marking of time, in the present-day churchyard stands a sundial base made from a column from one of the Roman temples.

One of the most important uses of the state religion was as an aid to military morale and discipline and as a means of uniting an army composed of legions drawn from hundreds of different tribes and races. A papyrus roll from a fort on the Upper Euphrates gives details of the festivals to be observed by the army throughout the year, noting all the services and sacrifices that were required.[5] The most important festival was that of Jupiter on 1st January when new altars were dedicated to the god on all the parade grounds of the Empire. The old ones were buried, as at Birdoswald on the Roman wall where nineteen altars dedicated by Dacian soldiers from Rumania have been found.

Once the due rites had been paid to the gods of the state and the Emperor, the Romans had a remarkably ecumenical attitude to religion. The savagery with which they put down druidism is more owed to their fear of it as a political force (and to their dislike of human sacrifice) than to any strictly dogmatic or religious grounds. This toleration of the native cults led to a fusion of beliefs which appears in the style and flavour of the best Romano–British art, notably at Bath.

The hot springs of Bath had been under the care of a Celtic goddess, Sul. The Romans at an early stage in their occupation used Bath, or Aquae Sulis as they called it, as a convalescent centre for sick legionaries. Around the sacred spring of Sul, now beneath the later King's Bath, there grew up a resplendent series of buildings connected either with worship or with healing or with both. They identified Sul with Minerva and built a magnificent classical temple to this composite goddess. Remains of the pediment can be seen in the Bath Museum, most notably the Medusa head, the emblem on Minerva's shield which the Celtic artist converted to a male moustachioed head with a wild sad expression. Other reminiscences of the place's use as a sacred site are the numbers of votive offerings thrown into the spring by worshippers; these include over 3,000 coins and twenty lead tablets invoking the goddess's curses on rivals or enemies. The most notable part of the complex to survive is the Great Bath, now open to the air but once, from the second century onward, covered by a gigantic barrel-vault made of hollow tiles to lessen the weight and rising to more than 50 ft. The altars and memorials show that visitors came from France and Germany as well as from nearer home for the solace and healing spirit one can still feel beside the Great Bath.

The strength of the native religious traditions is shown not only at Bath but right throughout the period of Roman occupation. At Lydney in Gloucestershire in the latter years of the fourth century a temple complex was built dedicated to the Celtic god Nodens, a god of hunting and the sea who was also regarded as a powerful healer. The temple was set beside a guest-house and a building where the patients and suppliants probably spent the night in hope of a dream or a visitation from the god. This last feature connects the rites here with those of the Greek god of healing, Aesculapius, and of Egyptian practices in which sleep and dreams were considered of the greatest therapeutic value.

The state religion of Rome provided for the social and family needs of the Empire. It could not provide for the deeper spiritual hunger of men and women looking for inner release, for certainty, for hope of immortality. These in various forms were provided in the classical world by the mystery religions, among the most notable of which were those of Cybele, Isis, and Mithras. It would seem that there was a temple of the Egyptian goddess Isis in London and the triangular temple at Verulamium, from the furnishings found during its excavations, has been identified as a shrine of the Mother Goddess Cybele, the object of wild and ecstatic rites. Her priests would castrate themselves in her honour. We have much fuller evidence of the worship of Mithras, partly because his cult was particularly popular in the Roman Army. Mithraism, which stems from the Persian religion of Zoroastrianism, was a Sun religion imported into the Empire in the first century BC. Mithras, depicted as a beautiful young man wearing a Phrygian cap, was a god of the Zoroastrian pantheon and was frequently addressed as *Sol invictus*, the unconquered Sun. He was born from a rock and in the course of his adventures he seized and sacrificed a huge bull by which he won salvation for mankind. This bull sacrifice is frequently depicted in art, notably in the sculptures found associated with the Temple of Mithras, the Mithraeum, discovered in London in 1954 and moved to a nearby site in the open air in Queen Victoria Street to enable it to be reconstructed and preserved. It is well worth while going to see it. Once it stood close to the Walbrook, a stream held sacred by the Celts who would fling sacrificial heads into its waters. Now its mysteries are bared to the vulgar and the curious where once masked devotees wearing the heads of birds and beasts struck awe into the hearts of initiates.

Another Mithraeum exists at Carrawburgh on Hadrian's Wall. This stands close to the sacred spring of the Celtic nymph Coventina. This Mithraeum was founded soon after AD 205 and it was probably desecrated by Christians in the early fourth century after the proclamation by the British-born Emperor Constantine of Christianity as the state religion of the Empire. The stern demands of the cult in terms of physical and moral courage and its stages of initiation through seven grades won by ordeals and tests would have won the adherence of many soldiers. The ordeal pit in which devotees were subjected to extremes of heat and cold may still be seen at Carrawburgh.

Mithraism was a cult for men alone. It was looked on with favour during the later years of the Empire because its adherents never refused the sacrifices and oaths of the official state religion. This was what the Christians insisted, in their extraordinary way, on doing. They invited martyrdom and terrible sufferings by their recusancy: the most notable example of this attitude is that of the protomartyr of Britain, St Alban.

Apart from the legendary stories of Glastonbury (to which we will return later) the earliest sign of Christianity coming to these islands is recorded by the Venerable Bede who says that in about AD 167 a British king called Lucius wrote to the Pope of the time, Eleutherius, asking to become a Christian.[6] The earliest archaeological evidence of Christianity comes from Manchester, dated to later in the same century. Until recently it was generally thought that St Alban suffered

65 St Albans, Hertford-
shire. A view between a
gap in the Roman walls of
Verulamium, looking
towards a lake formed by
the waters of the river Ver,
showing the tower and
nave roof of St Alban's
Abbey, the site of the
protomartyr's execution.
The Norman tower was
built of Roman bricks
taken from Verulamium.

under the Diocletian persecutions in 303. It is now thought that his martyrdom
took place during the reign of the Emperor Septimius Severus on 22 June 209.[7]

Alban was a citizen of the important *municipium* of Verulamium. This had
been founded close to the capital of the British tribe, the Catuvellani, in AD 49 or
50. It was taken and burnt by Boudicca during her rebellion but was soon
rebuilt and enlarged, acquiring a forum and basilica, temples and a theatre. The
remarkable collections in the museum enable the visitor to form an excellent
picture of life at various stages in this prosperous city, especially in the present
context, of the style of life and belief against which St Alban so dramatically
rebelled.

According to the version of his martyrdom told by Bede, Alban was a pagan
who sheltered a Christian priest from persecution. He was converted by the
priest and when soldiers came to seize the priest, Alban, wearing the priest's
cloak, gave himself up instead of his guest. Led before the magistrate, he was
asked to make the customary sacrifices and refused. 'What is your family and
race?' demanded the judge. 'How does my family concern you?' replied Alban;
'if you wish to know the truth about my religion, know that I am a Christian,
and am bound by the laws of Christ.' 'I demand to know your name', insisted the
judge, 'tell me at once.' 'My parents named me Alban', he answered, 'and I
worship and adore the living and true God, who created all things.'[8] The
infuriated magistrate ordered him to be flogged and then, because Alban still
resisted, to be beheaded. Led to execution outside the city to the hill where his
abbey now stands, Alban came to the river Ver which could not be crossed
because of the crowd gathered on the bridge. At his prayer the waters of the Ver
parted and Alban and the soldiers crossed over and up the hill. The soldier

66 St Albans. The early fourteenth-century shrine of St Alban in the retrochoir of the abbey church. Shattered at the Dissolution, the shrine was painstakingly reconstructed in the last century.

appointed to execute him threw away his sword and begged to join him in martyrdom. At the summit of the hill Alban prayed for water and a spring bubbled up, granting his request. Then he was beheaded and the soldier who had refused to execute him was beheaded as well. As for the substitute executioner, his eyes dropped out of his head on to the ground. Bede says that the magistrate was so astounded by these miracles that he called a halt to the persecutions and was himself converted.

St Alban's fame spread abroad and lasted into the Dark Ages. His body was rediscovered in the eighth century by the Saxon King Offa who richly endowed the abbey. The present great church, the second longest in England, was built by the first Norman abbot, Paul of Caen, using Roman bricks from the ruins of Verulamium. The site of St Alban's shrine behind the high altar of the abbey church is one of the most moving and charged of all the places we consider here. The air sings with the words of Christ: 'Greater love hath no man than this, that he lay down his life for his friends', and about you rises the evidence of the civilizing force that derives from true sacrifice and fructifies throughout succeeding centuries the resources of art.

Chapter 5

Christian sites and shrines of the Dark Ages

67 Glastonbury, Somerset. The fifteenth-century tower of St Michael's Church on Glastonbury Tor. The line marking the spiral path of ascent may be seen clearly here.

Let us start with a legend—or rather, the two linked legends of Joseph of Arimathaea and of King Arthur which are both intimately connected with Glastonbury.[1] Both legends received their first full written record in the twelfth century but they drew on oral traditions of much greater antiquity. According to the first legend St Joseph of Arimathaea with a band of missionaries, sent by the Apostle Philip, brought the Christian faith to Britain in AD 63. He carried with him the Holy Grail, the cup used at the Last Supper in which he had caught drops of Christ's blood at the Crucifixion. Landing in Cornwall they travelled towards Glastonbury. When nearly there, on the hill called Wearyall, Joseph thrust his hawthorn staff into the ground and it immediately burst into blossom. He settled on the present site of the abbey ruins of Glastonbury and built there the first Christian church in Britain, made of wattle and daub. This *vetusta*

ecclesia or Ancient Church was said to have existed up to the great fire of 1184 when it was destroyed. In another version of the legend preserved amongst Cornish and Somerset miners Joseph had been to Glastonbury before, bringing with him the Virgin Mary and the young Jesus Christ who as a trained carpenter had built the church. It was upon this legend that William Blake drew for his poem *Jerusalem*, which has now become an alternative national anthem.

St Joseph was said to have buried the Grail in an unknown place near Glastonbury and this connects, of course, with the legend of King Arthur and his knights searching for the Holy Grail. Glastonbury came to be identified with Avalon, the island of apples to which Arthur was borne by the three black-robed queens after the last battle with Mordred. This association of Glastonbury with Arthur received a great boost in 1191 when a monk of the abbey, inspired by a

68 *Left, above* Glastonbury. The Chalice Well, a spring of great antiquity with its modern cover design influenced by the Celtic revival.

69 *Left* Glastonbury. The Glastonbury Thorn in flower. This branch is on one of several trees descending from the original, cut down at the Dissolution.

70 Glastonbury. The ruins of the thirteenth-century crossing of the abbey church, with, on the left, part of the nave.

vision, discovered the coffin of Arthur and Guenevere. The coffin bore on it an inscription 'Here lies the famous King Arthur buried in the Island of Avalon' and when opened it was found to contain the skeletons of the king and queen. The blonde tresses of Guenevere crumbled in the hand of a monk when he touched them.

It is not surprising that Glastonbury should be associated with such powerful legends. The whole landscape containing it is like a glossary of archetypal images—indeed a galaxy of such images if one pays attention to the theory that it is part of an immense depiction of the twelve signs of the zodiac formed by rising ground, streams, old roads, and field boundaries.[2] Originally surrounded by marsh and water, the 400-ft Tor with Chalice Hill and the site of the abbey and the town westwards all formed an island, and seen from a distance on a misty day or evening from the neighbouring hills, they still give the impression of insularity. Not far away were the lake villages of Celts of the La Tène culture and it is thought that Glastonbury was their island of the dead, though so far no cemetery has been discovered. Following this thought, it is supposed that the Celtic Christian monks who first founded a settlement here were inspired to make this ancient holy place a hallowed site of the new faith. It has also been suggested that the Tor itself, a strange cone now crowned by the tower of the medieval church of St Michael, was, from the Bronze Age or before, a site of initiation, a three-dimensional maze traced by a spiral path about its sides.

A usual pattern for visitors is to go to the abbey ruins first of all, then to the Chalice Well, and last to climb the Tor. Few of the ruins brought about by the Dissolution of the Monasteries produce such a pang as do these of Glastonbury, whether because the surviving parts of the Lady Chapel and St Joseph's Chapel and of the transepts are enough to make us realize what a great composite work of art was destroyed here or whether because the whole site smarts with the pain of the psychic damage that was done to England with the sudden and violent denial of the contemplative tradition in the expulsion of the monks. Excavations here have shown traces of the original Celtic monastic settlement, first recorded as already existing in 658. Traditions maintain that St Patrick, St Brigid and St David all visited this monastery. Refounded by Ine of Wessex, the abbey began its great period in 940 under an energetic abbot, Dunstan, later to be Archbishop of Canterbury. None of the Celtic or Anglo-Saxon remains are visible: what you see are the ruins of the great church built after the fire of 1181, largely in the Transitional and Early English styles. There is of course the famous Abbot's Kitchen and a descendant of Joseph of Arimathaea's original hawthorn, which confirms all the legends about it by blooming at Christmas-time.

On the way to the Tor is the Chalice Well, lined with ancient stonework worked in a way which prompted Sir Flinders Petrie to suggest that it was built by Egyptian traders. Under the guidance of the mystic and writer, the late Major Tudor Pole, this has been restored and maintained. Then you may begin the ascent of the Tor, which has already intrigued you by its shape and position, and you ascend to the summit where Richard Whiting, last abbot of Glastonbury, was executed as a traitor in 1539 at Henry VIII's command. There is a spirit about this place, conveyed by the fine air, the views of the intense blue colours of the Somerset countryside, the sense of being taken up above the world, that is most special. Perhaps it is connected with the dedication of the church, whose tower only remains, to the Archangel Michael, the vanquisher of evil, and perhaps every visitor here in climbing the Tor has climbed some way up the mystical hill of the soul and found some release, some sense of a peace that is above the turmoil of passing time.

An Arthurian site visible from Glastonbury Tor is the hillfort of South Cadbury, traditionally said to be the site of King Arthur's Camelot.[3] This is an Iron Age hillfort reoccupied and fortified not only in the period of King Arthur but also in later Anglo-Saxon times. The sites associated with King Arthur range up and down the country, from Tintagel where he was born, known to have been a most important Celtic monastery in the Early Dark Ages, to Arthur's Seat in Edinburgh. The Arthur we think of today is a figure symbolizing the defence of Christian civilization and the establishment of earthly rule on a basis of justice and compassion: he and the legends surrounding his knights and his court on the one hand derive from traditions and beliefs going far back into the pagan Celtic era and even further beyond[4] and on the other hand are seen through the screen of later medieval chivalric society. The Arthur of South Cadbury–Camelot, who defeated the Anglo-Saxons at the great battle of Mons Badonicus in 494, traditionally on the site of Liddington Castle near Swindon, must, by nature of the evidence, have been far more local and provincial in his outlook. Nevertheless he would seem to have saved Romano-Christian culture at a time when it was threatened with extinction by the Anglo-Saxon advance.

From the departure of the Roman legions in 410 up to the arrival of St Augustine and his missionaries in Kent in 597 the Anglo-Saxons were impervious to Christianity. They remained true to their gods, Woden and the other deities of the Northern pantheon, and Celtic Christianity made no impact on them. The state of hostility between the races made conversion impossible. What the Christian Romano–British, holding a line stretching from Dorset up to Strathclyde in Scotland up to the time of their defeat at Dyrham in the mid-sixth

71 *Above* Whitesand Bay, Dyfed. From this bay near St Davids, St Patrick returned to Ireland to convert the pagan Irish. The site of his chapel is marked by a plaque.

72 *Overleaf, left* Rock of Cashel, Tipperary. Inside Cormac's Chapel, one of the masterworks of Irish Romanesque, built under Rhineland influence in about 1120.

73 *Overleaf, right* St Ninian's cave, Whithorn, Dumfries and Galloway, used in the early fifth century as a cell by St Ninian for his devotions. Crosses inscribed on its rocky walls are said to go back to the eighth century.

century, did was to convert the pagans in the remote areas of Cornwall and Wales which had been touched to a far less extent than the eastern regions of Britain by Roman influence and then to convert Ireland and those parts of Scotland which the Romans had never conquered. With these times we enter the Age of the Saints.

The process of conversion had begun shortly before the Roman withdrawal. In 397 St Ninian introduced Christianity to Scotland. He had been on pilgrimage to Rome and came to Whithorn in Galloway where he built a small stone church covered with white plaster. Remains of a building corresponding to this description have been uncovered in excavations. These are now covered over and the visible remains are of the thirteenth-century Premonstratensian priory. The museum contains the Latinus Stone of 450, the earliest record of Christianity in Scotland. Three miles away on the coast can be seen St Ninian's cave, which he used as an oratory. Inside the cave and on the rocks outside votive crosses are carved which are said to go back to the eighth century. The complete conversion of Scotland to Christianity was carried out by Irish missionaries nearly two hundred years later.

Christians had come first to Ireland escaping from barbarian invasions on the continent: notable among them was St Declan of Ardmore. By 431 there were enough Christian converts for Rome to appoint a bishop for them. It was at about this time that St Patrick, a native of Cumbria who had spent some time in Ireland as a slave after being captured by pirates, returned there on his great mission. He had managed to escape from captivity, going first to Gaul and then coming to Wales. It was from the beautiful Whitesand Bay outside St Davids that he set sail, arriving near Downpatrick. Most of his work was carried out in the

74 Station Island, Donegal. The modern church and pilgrimage centre on this island in Lough Derg where, in a cave known as St Patrick's Purgatory, the saint experienced the three worlds of the afterlife. The cave was sealed up in the late Middle Ages and its present whereabouts are unknown.

northern parts of Ireland, from his seat at Armagh, but he travelled throughout the island. What comes through from his few written remains and from the many legends about him is the power of a personality devoted wholly to the Christian message; it must have been the force of his nature as in the scenes already described at the Hill of Slane and Tara that made his mission so immediately effective in the conversion of the kings of Ireland despite the opposition of their druids. One of the most notable sites associated with such a conversion is Cashel. This rock rising out of the plain of Tipperary is now ringed by a great wall containing a cathedral, a castle built into the cathedral nave, a round tower, and one of the greatest works of the Irish Romanesque, Cormac's Chapel. The young King of Munster, Aengus, hearing of Patrick's arrival, had gone with joy to greet him and to ask for baptism. On the Rock of Cashel at the spot marked until recently by a twelfth-century cross, Patrick baptized Aengus. During the ceremony Aengus' foot was pierced by the sharp point of the staff on which Patrick was leaning; afterwards Patrick, noticing his staff still driven into Aengus' foot, asked why he had not protested—to which the king replied that he thought the wounding was part of the ceremony.

St Patrick's conversion of the ruling classes had obvious practical benefits in securing his success; on a wider scale it led to the happy and fertile fusion between Christianity and Celtic tradition that was to flower for hundreds of years in the manuscripts, metalwork, sculpture and architecture of Ireland. In preaching the Trinity to the Irish people, Patrick found minds already prepared by centuries of the Celtic veneration for the number three. Later legends tell of Patrick's conversations with ancient heroes such as Caoilte and Oisin brought back from the dead in which they debate the differences between the old and the new worlds. (See Chapter 3.)

Such an influence stemming from Celtic stories of other worlds may lie behind St Patrick's visit to Lough Derg in Donegal where on Station Island he descended into a cave and experienced visions of the three worlds of the afterlife, Hell, Purgatory, and Heaven. Pilgrims in later years would return from Lough Derg, reporting that they too had experienced these visions, and the twelfth-century account of the Knight Owen spread round Europe and may well have been one of the seminal influences on Dante's *Divine Comedy*.[5] Such excesses of drunkenness and other vices were committed by later pilgrims that the cave was sealed up and its site is no longer known. Sober and fasting pilgrims still make the journey to Station Island.

St Patrick died in 461 and was buried at Downpatrick in a grave where his body was later joined by those of St Brigid and St Columba. Though he had introduced the episcopal administration of the Church, the path the Celtic Church followed in Ireland was far more influenced by Eastern monasticism. The rule of the first monks in the Egyptian desert was brought to Ireland by way of Marseilles and Tours, and it integrated better with native Irish customs. In many cases the monastery once founded became the possession of a particular tribe; on conversion the tribal leader was sometimes made the first abbot and his successors were of his own kin. Thus members of the same family occupied the chair of St Patrick at Armagh for two centuries and the first eleven successors of St Columba at Iona were all of his family. The same custom also applied in Wales. The disadvantage of this could be that the animosity that was traditionally felt and expressed between tribes was now transferred to the monasteries. Far more monasteries were besieged and sacked in inter-abbatial rivalries than ever in the raids of the Norsemen. That however applies in general to a later period. Many of the early monasteries such as that founded by St Kevin at Glendalough in the sixth century became noted centres of learning and the arts. Glendalough, seated between two lakes in the midst of the Wicklow mountains, retains to an exceptional degree a number of churches and remains from a very early period up to the twelfth century when its see was transferred to Dublin. Beside the Upper Lake, reachable only by boat, is St Kevin's Bed, a cave to which the saint retired when in need of seclusion for his prayers.

What these early monks would do to find freedom to pray and contemplate is shown at its most extreme at the island of Skellig Michael, eight miles off the south-west Irish coast. Here the beehive cells of the monastery testify to the heroic disregard of bodily sufferings or rather the inviting of them as the monks strove to dispossess their inner natures of personal desires and thoughts in their

75 Glendalough, Wicklow. The church and round tower known as St Kevin's Kitchen, one of the many surviving church and other remains in this famous monastery. It is dated variously between the ninth and twelfth centuries.

surrender to divine contemplations. Great numbers of monastic sites, often in more kindly surroundings, survive such as that of Clonmacnois, the foundation of St Ciaran beside the River Shannon, or the not distant oratory of St Flannan beside the cathedral of Killaloe. In such monasteries much of permanent value from the ancient world was preserved for Western civilization. The saints and monks loved learning and in their desire for the experience of the divine worlds they would appear to have transcended the mere desire for knowledge and changed what they knew by changing themselves. In a remarkably few years they were returning to the mainland of Europe the gifts they had received. Around AD 600 St Columbanus was founding monasteries in France and Italy, St Gall founded one of the most influential of all Dark Age monasteries in Switzerland, and St Fergil became bishop of Salzburg. The spirit of these early

76 Skellig Michael, off Kerry. A cross (c. AD 800) between beehive cells of the monastery established on the largest of a group of islands, eight miles from the mainland.

monks is conveyed in many poems such as this tenth-century one called 'The wish of Manchán of Liath':

> I wish, O son of the Living God, ancient eternal King, for a secret hut in the wilderness that it may be my dwelling.
>
> A very blue shallow well to be beside it, a clear pool for washing away sins through the grace of the Holy Ghost.
>
> A beautiful wood close by around it on every side, for the nurture of many-voiced birds, to shelter and hide it.[6]

The travelling saint we are next concerned with journeyed unwillingly. This is St Columba (or Columcille). In 563, when he was 41, he left Ireland in penance for unwittingly causing a war by copying out a Vulgate belonging to

77 Iona, Inner Hebrides. The holy island of St Columba: a view of the cathedral looking across the sound to Mull.

his old tutor Finnian of Moville. He had already in Ireland established the two noted monasteries of Derry and Durrow. Accompanied by twelve disciples he sailed north and came to the island of I, now known as Iona. On landing he climbed a hill to make sure he could not see Ireland and would therefore not be tempted even by a shadow of his homeland on the water. This hill is still known as the 'Hill of the back to Ireland'. Here on Iona he founded a monastery from which for thirty-four years he worked for the conversion of Scotland.

Iona is tiny. Three and a half miles long, with white sandy beaches and soft green hillocks out of which rise ancient mounds, stones, and the fine cathedral, it is in most noted contrast to the volcanic and frightening landscape of Mull off which it lies. Its smallness adds to the intensity of the experience of going there and to the feeling Dr Johnson expressed to Boswell: 'That man is little to be

envied, whose patriotism would not gain force upon the plain of Marathon, or whose piety would not grow warmer among the ruins of Iona.'[7] Known earlier as the Island of the Druids, it possesses sacred wells which were probably the scenes of earlier rites before Columba's coming, as well as a big grassy mound known as Sithean Mor, 'the great mound of the fairies' or else as 'The Hill of the Angels' because, as St Adamnan records, Columba was praying here when he was visited by bands of angels in white garments who flew down to converse with him.

Not many remains survive of Columba's own time though his cell and his bed of stone have been uncovered in recent times. The cathedral is largely of the early sixteenth century, incorporating a twelfth-century Benedictine nunnery. An ancient oratory which held the shrine of St Columba is attached to the north-

78 Skellig Michael. A stone cross and beehive cells: a reverse view from that in plate 76.

79 *Above right* Iona. The tenth-century St Martin's Cross standing near the cathedral is one of the few survivors of the 360 crosses that once stood on St Columba's island.

west corner of the nave. Before the west door of the cathedral stands St Martin's Cross and a replica of one of the finest of all Celtic crosses, that of St John. The original was unfortunately shattered in a gale. These are among the few remnants of the 360 crosses which once adorned the island and which were thrown into the sea at the Reformation. Leading to the cathedral is the Street of the Dead and the mounds where sixty kings of Scotland, Ireland, and Norway were buried. The atmosphere of the island is still Columba's.

Delightful I think it to be in the bosom of an isle, on the peak of a rock, that I might often see there the calm of the sea.

That I might see its heavy waves over the glittering ocean, as they chant a melody to their Father on their eternal course.

80 *Above* St Michael's Mount, Cornwall, on which the Archangel Michael appeared to some fishermen in AD 495. There are many remains of the later monastery.

81 *Left* Birsay, Orkney. The ruins of the first cathedral of Orkney built by a Viking earl. The see was transferred to Kirkwall after the martyrdom of St Magnus in 1117.

82 *Right* Corfe Castle, Dorset. Ruins of the medieval castle built on a site associated with the martyrdom of the Saxon king Edward, murdered by his step-mother in 979.

83 Dunadd, Argyll. The path St Columba must have trodden up to the site of the citadel or nuclear fort of the Scotic kings of Dalriada.

That I might see its smooth strand of clear headlands, no gloomy thing; that I might hear the voice of the wondrous birds, a joyful tune.

That I might hear the sound of the shallow waves against the rocks; that I might hear the cry by the graveyard, the noise of the sea.

That I might see its splendid flocks of birds over the full-watered ocean; that I might see its mighty whales, greatest of wonders.

That I might see its ebb and its flood-tide in their flow; that this might be my name, a secret I tell, 'He who turned his back on Ireland.'[8]

From here Columba travelled across Scotland, meeting St Mungo who was busy at work converting the people of Strathclyde, going to Dunadd, the seat of the Scotic kings of Dalriada, and founding Christian settlements on the mainland. He died on Iona in 597, the very year in which Augustine brought Roman Christianity to the distant Jutes of Kent. The influence of Iona spread far, not only in Scotland but also throughout the North of England. Lindisfarne, the great Northumbrian monastery, was the creation of a monk from Iona, St Aidan, 'the candle of the north', and it is with the meeting and merging of the strands of Celtic and Roman Christianity that we are next concerned.

The return of Britain to connexion with the centre of Western Catholic Christianity in Rome was the work of St Gregory the Great who became Pope in 591. Though he never came to Britain he had the profoundest effect on that part of our story that remains to be told, for several reasons. On the strength of his spirituality, his learning, his political sense and his personality he raised the Papacy to a new height of authority, one from which it often declined but which remained a point of reference for all his successors. By establishing the patrimony of Peter, the papal lands in Italy, he began the role of the Papacy as a temporal ruler. By reformulating and organizing the Church's teaching on the subject of the saints and martyrs known as the doctrine of the treasury of intercession, he gave a new and orthodox impulse to the needs of men and women for intermediaries between themselves and the deity, something that obviously had a deep effect on the founding of many holy places. By starting a missionary movement in sending St Augustine to Britain, he began the process that, lasting long after his death, led to the conversion of Teutonic and Scandinavian Europe to Christianity. Bede says that his interest in the Anglo-Saxons was aroused before he became Pope by the sight of blonde Angle children on sale as slaves in Rome.[9]

Gregory had wanted to lead a mission to Britain himself but was refused permission by the Pope. When he himself was raised to the Papacy, he chose his close associate Augustine to lead a mission of forty monks. Augustine set off in 596 but was so disturbed by the dangers of venturing amongst pagan barbarians of whose language he and his companions were ignorant that he delayed on the journey until urged on by letter from Gregory.

Augustine and his companions landed on the Isle of Thanet off the Kentish coast. The King of Kent was Ethelbert whose wife Bertha was Christian, being a Frankish princess. The king met them with some reserve at first, refusing to greet them in a house in case they practised magical arts on him. He allowed them to preach and to make conversions, giving them somewhere to live in the ancient Roman city of Canterbury where they restored the Romano–British church of St Martin. The example of their lives inspired many conversions, the most important of which was that of Ethelbert who gave them the land for the abbey of Christ Church and the site of the present cathedral. Augustine went to France to be consecrated Archbishop of this new province of the Church. More will be said of Canterbury later, especially in relation to St Thomas à Becket, but here I must note that one of the most moving moments in the recent visit of Pope John Paul II was when he and the Archbishop of Canterbury greeted each other in the present cathedral as the heirs respectively of St Gregory the Great and of St Augustine of Canterbury.

Gregory continued to take a great interest in the success of the mission, and one of the most important documents for our purposes is his instructions to Augustine on what to do with the heathen places of worship. This he set out in a letter to the Abbot Mellitus who was to become the first bishop of London. He had decided that the pagan temples of the Anglo-Saxons should on no account be destroyed. The idols in them should be done away but the temples should be sprinkled with holy water and altars with relics enclosed in them should be set up. 'In this way we hope that the people, seeing that its temples are not destroyed, may abandon idolatry and resort to these places as before, and may come to know and adore the true God.'[10] He also says that as they have the custom of sacrificing oxen to devils, some other festivity should be substituted in its place, a day of Dedication or of the Festivals of the Martyrs whose relics are preserved in the altars. They are to construct shelters of boughs around their former temples and celebrate with devout feasting. 'They are no longer to sacrifice beasts to the Devil, but they may kill them for food to the praise of God, and give thanks to the Giver of all gifts for his bounty. If the people are allowed some worldly pleasures in this way, they will more readily come to desire the joys of the spirit.'[11]

Thus in these wise and gentle instructions we see one of the most formative elements in the making of our holy places and in the continuity that they embody between the changes of religion, of civilization, and of races. The same practice had been followed by the Celtic saints but here was the greatest spiritual leader of the West lending his authority to a practice that helped to soothe one of the most difficult transitions the psyches of our forebears have had to endure. In the course of the Dark Ages under the influence of Christianity there took place a revolution in the attitude of man to nature and his environment as far-reaching as the Neolithic change from societies based on hunting to societies based on farming or the introduction of the close communities of cities. The effect of Christianity was to abolish or to drive underground the love and worship and fear which men and women paid to the tutelary deities of nature and the home. This came about at the same time as the introduction of the heavy plough drawn by oxen which enabled men to till the earth to a greater depth than ever before and to extract in bigger yields the energy latent in the earth. Released from fearing the anger of the spirits of wood, stone, and forest, man was effectively licensed to hack, carve, and delve as he pleased. As a mediating force between himself and the Godhead he was allowed, by the doctrine of the treasury of intercession, instead of these tutelary deities, to pray to the Virgin and to the saints, whether his local or regional saint, or else saints entrusted with special duties or powers. Many of these last saints took over the functions of older deities and many assumed in their legends past and ancient traditions from their pagan predecessors.

As the early saints died and miracles were reported at their shrines, so these shrines became the foci of local patriotism, an emotion that had been expressed earlier through the war ethos of the tribe and that had often centred in the case of the Anglo-Saxons on the semi-divine nature of their kings who claimed descent from Woden. The strong individualism and marked personalities of these saints stand out in severe contrast to the tribalism of the races they converted. These tribes were as institutions guided by myths from the ancient past; the very concept of law amongst the Anglo-Saxons was that of the doom, something that could only be interpreted, not altered. The role of the individual mattered only in that he was a part of the tribe. The missionaries who came from other societies broke through the enclosed and parochial nature of the tribe, bringing the hope of a way of life that could develop and change the individual personality, offering the idea of conscience as the light of inner emotional truth, and at the same time revealing the attractions of an international civilization in learning and the arts of an order far different from the blood-hungry legends of the Teutonic past. The missionaries exhibited time and again the one quality the Anglo-Saxons prized above all others: courage. And just as St Patrick drew on the Irish veneration for the number three, so the missionaries in England found in telling the story of the Crucifixion minds already prepared by the legend of Woden sacrificing himself to himself upon the tree,[12] a myth perhaps underlying the great Anglo-Saxon poem 'The dream of the Rood', quotations from which were carved on the Ruthwell Cross.

The impact of Christianity on Anglo-Saxon pagan society is well shown in the conversion by St Paulinus of the great King Edwin of Northumbria. Edwin had married a daughter of Ethelbert of Kent. She had been allowed to bring Paulinus with her as her confessor. Much pressure was brought by Paulinus to bear on Edwin who, as Bede says, was a wise and prudent man who often sat alone in silence for long periods, wondering which religion he should follow. After much reflection he told Paulinus he wished to consult his court. His High Priest, Coifi,

84 *Below* Ruthwell, Dumfries and Galloway. A detail of the shaft of the Ruthwell cross (AD 670–750) showing (*left*) Christ with the Magdalen anointing His feet and (*right*) beasts in swirling ornamentation. The cross is carved with Latin and runic inscriptions.

85 *Right* Monasterboice, Louth. The cross of Muiredach, the most richly carved of all the Irish standing crosses (*c.* AD 900) showing the crucifixion with scenes from the life of Christ in the panels below.

at the meeting, recommended acceptance of Christianity and another courtier said that if Christianity could tell them more about what goes before this life and what follows it better than the old religion, then they should follow it. He compared the brief life of man on earth to the flight of a sparrow through the king's mead-hall in the winter. After Coifi had asked to hear more from Paulinus, he himself volunteered to be the first to desecrate the temples of the religion of which he was the chief representative. Then carrying a spear and riding a stallion (both acts forbidden to a priest of his religion) he went to the temple at Goodmanham (east of York) and hurled his spear at the temple and ordered it to be burnt.[13] The great Minster of York rises on the site of the holy well where Paulinus baptized Edwin.

Thus the Northumbrians adopted Christianity. Edwin however was to be

86 York Minster. A view of the thirteenth-century south transept and the west towers of this great cathedral that includes in its foundations the site of the baptism of Edwin of Northumbria by Paulinus.

87 Lindisfarne, North-umberland. Ruins of the medieval monastery refounded on the site of St Aidan's monastery centuries after eighty years of Viking raids (AD 793–875) forced the monks of the first foundation to flee. Lindisfarne castle, restored by Sir Edwin Lutyens, is on the right.

killed by the ferocious pagan King Penda of the Mercians and Paulinus was forced to return south. Edwin's successor, the saint and martyr Oswald, in wishing to revive northern Christianity turned to Iona rather than Canterbury. The community sent a monk who was not well received and who returned in disgust. In discussing what had gone wrong with his mission another monk, Aidan, voiced criticisms of his approach and, while he spoke, it dawned on his companions that Aidan should be sent. Aidan formed a great friendship with Oswald and founded his monastery on the tidal island of Lindisfarne within sight of the king's fortress of Bamburgh on its proud rock overlooking the North Sea.

This long low green island, with the Farne Islands as outriders, preserves the ruins of the later medieval monastery. One of its first bishops was St Cuthbert who as a shepherd boy on the Lammermuir Hills in 651 saw a vision of angels

88 Durham. The towers of the cathedral seen from the west, above the river Wear. The Lady Chapel known as the Galilee extends from the west front.

bearing St Aidan's soul to heaven. Inspired by that vision he joined the monastic community at Melrose Abbey under its founder Eata. Eata took Cuthbert with him to be the guestmaster at Ripon and then to Lindisfarne where he made Cuthbert prior. Cuthbert longed for solitude and was given permission to retire to the Great Farne Island where he lived in a sunken turf oratory. Many stories are told of his affection for the birds and other creatures there—a characteristic of his earlier life when he was once seen to enter the sea to pray and when two seals came to dry his feet with their fur. He was forced to issue from his retreat when he was consecrated bishop and had to fulfil his new duties. When he felt the approach of death, however, he returned to the beloved solitude of his island where he died in 687. On removing his body to Lindisfarne the monks were surprised to find that it was incorrupt. His body remained at Lindisfarne until the

89 Hexham, North-umberland. The Frith Stool or the stone *cathedra* of St Wilfred in the thirteenth-century choir of Hexham Abbey, which also includes the crypt of Wilfred's church in its foundations.

Viking attack on the Abbey in 875 when the monks in fleeing took it with them together with the head of St Oswald and the relics of St Aidan. These relics were kept at Chester le Street for over a hundred years until later Viking attacks forced the monks to move again. They came south, guided it is said by the body of the saint which refused to be lifted if they were about to go in the wrong direction, and came to the present great hill of Durham where they built the church now superseded by the cathedral, one of the greatest architectural achievements of Europe.

Cuthbert's life had bridged the time of the reconciliation of the Roman and the Celtic Churches in Britain. St Augustine had attempted to make friends with the Celtic Bishops of the West and had failed, partly because of his own rudeness in refusing to rise from his chair when they met. The long separation of the Celtic

Christians from Europe and their use of a different method for calculating the date of Easter had led to a sharp division between the branches of the Church. This was settled at the Synod of Whitby in 664 when the quarrelsome St Wilfred used his forensic talents to defeat the Celtic opposition in debate, after which monks and priests like St Cuthbert, brought up in the Celtic tradition, accepted the Roman ways. St Wilfred is associated with three notable holy places, Ripon and Hexham in the north and Selsey on the Sussex coast in the south. Ripon and Hexham both retain the crypts of his original churches and at Hexham his chair, known as the Frith Stool, stands in the body of the Church, possibly in the very same place as in his day. Exiled from Northumbria after he had become bishop at York because of a quarrel, he went to Rome for redress for his grievances and also during this period he went to the South Saxons who were among the last of their race to be converted to Christianity. No remains apart from the chancel of a later church may be seen beside the secluded sea lake at Selsey with its view of the cathedral of Chichester to which his see was later transferred.

Our chief record of these times we owe to one of the greatest Englishmen, the theologian and historian the Venerable Bede, who at the age of seven was placed by his parents in the monastery of St Peter at Monkwearmouth which had been founded by the cultivated and widely travelled Benedict Biscop. The churches and sites at Monkwearmouth and at Jarrow to which Bede later moved are to be visited and revered, both for the very early Anglo-Saxon architecture that survives there and for their association with Benedict Biscop and with Bede. To Benedict Biscop we owe the revival of architecture in England: of noble family, he was educated on the continent to which he returned on several occasions, most notably on visits to Rome. He brought back with him vestments, altar

90 *Below left* Monk-wearmouth, Tyne and Wear. An arched doorway surviving from the early Anglo-Saxon church. Here the Venerable Bede spent his early days as a monk.

91 *Below right* Durham. The Galilee or Lady Chapel of the cathedral, built in the Transitional style *c.* 1170, which contains (*right*) the tomb of the Venerable Bede.

vessels and paintings and also engaged stonemasons and glaziers in Gaul to teach their crafts to the Northumbrians. He also brought the Archcantor of St Peter's in Rome to teach his monks the Roman liturgical chant. In addition to his taste and patronage he was a most learned man. From his endeavours can be traced the great traditions of English ecclesiastical architecture which were to add so much to the beauty and the hallowed atmosphere of our holy places. To Bede we owe something else that affects our feeling for their atmosphere and that is memory in the form of written history. For the first time, our history was recorded, with all the care in the selection of sources that had gone to make the great classical models on which Bede drew, by someone who was a native of these islands. A scholar to the last, he died in 735 after dictating the last chapter of a book he had been working on. Bede was buried at Monkwearmouth, but in 1020 his bones were stolen by a monk and taken to Durham where they now lie in a great stone altar tomb, in the western chapel known as the Galilee.

Just as Irish missionaries had earlier taken their learning and missionary zeal to the continent, so the Anglo-Saxons were to export saints. St Boniface and St Willibrord undertook the conversion of Germany where they were to be followed later by one of the chief ornaments of Northumbrian civilization, Alcuin, who led the renaissance of learning at the court of Charlemagne.

The civilization of Northumbria was to be destroyed in the Viking invasions, of which more will be said later. More must be said of Celtic and Pictish Christianity both before and after the Synod of Whitby had in general settled the quarrel between the Celtic and Roman Churches.

Cornwall remained a separate Celtic enclave until her conquest by Athelstan in the tenth century, but with close connexions with Brittany, Wales, and Ireland, all of which sent missionaries for the conversion of the Cornish. They received archangelic help in 495 when St Michael appeared to some fishermen on the tidal island that bears his name. St Michael's Mount, which was probably a holy place in pre-Christian times, was to become the chief shrine of Cornwall, acquiring a monastery of which much, including the church and ancient crosses, remains to be visited today. The saint most venerated by the Cornish was St Piran who was popularly supposed to have discovered tin and was thus the founder of the tin-mining of the peninsula. He arrived in Cornwall in 480 miraculously floating with a millstone about his neck; it had been placed there by enemies who had thrown him over a cliff. A very early church was uncovered from under the sands at Perranzabuloe in the last century but it has now been covered again to save its remnants from the vandalism of modern tourists. St Piran's strange method of sea travel was paralleled by many other saints. My own patron St Uny of Lelant arrived from Ireland floating on a stone; his sister St Eia who founded St Ives showed her greater holiness by floating on an oak leaf. As for St Warna who used the more conventional conveyance of a coracle, she nevertheless braved the Western Rocks of the Isles of Scilly and disembarked safely in a cove 'where none but the canonized should attempt to land'.

No Cornish Bede recorded their exploits and the names are largely unknown to the hagiographers of Rome. The stories about them were mostly handed down by word of mouth until they were collected in the last century.[14] Numerous churches and villages together with holy wells, crosses, and other sites are named after them, reflecting the local patriotism their memories aroused. The very humbleness of the way in which their memory persists adds another dimension to our understanding of the impact of Christianity on ancient pagan societies. It was the force of their individuality that made their memories live in folk memories and still live in those who love the stories of them, like the legend of St Nectan, whose silver bell used to ring out to sea from his secluded valley near Tintagel, making the fishermen prostrate themselves in worship. After his death, this bell was buried under a stream with the body of the saint by strange foreign ladies who then starved to death in his cell. The bell will never be heard until there is peace in warring Christendom.

The close connexion of saints' names with healing wells shows a clear continuity with the Celtic veneration of water. This is shown most definitely with the added image of the severed head at Holywell in North Wales. Here St Winifride was beheaded by a Prince Caradoc who was enraged at her refusing his advances: where her head touched the ground a well burst forth. St Beuno, after cursing Caradoc who fell dead, placed Winifride's head back on her shoulders and she stood up alive and well. Later St Beuno took her to the well and declared that all who prayed for her help there would have their wish granted. The present building housing the well was built by Lady Margaret Beaufort in about 1500. It is best known through the lovely fragments of a play about St Winifride by Gerard Manley Hopkins, and very suitably the shrine is in the care of his brother Jesuits today. It is remarkable also in that no other centre of pilgrimage in Britain can show such an unbroken continuity as Holywell, such was the strength of feeling it provoked amongst Catholics in all the worst years of persecution and recusancy. A not dissimilar story is told of the saint of Oxford, St Frideswide. Pursued to Binsey by an amorous Saxon, she prayed to St Margaret of Antioch who first struck the Saxon blind and then caused a spring to burst forth with whose waters Frideswide cured the blindness of her now repentant admirer.

92 *Left* Binsey, near Oxford. The holy well that gushed forth at the prayer of St Frideswide to St Margaret of Antioch in the churchyard at Binsey.

93 *Right* Ahenny, Tipperary. One of two early crosses dated to the eighth century because of the resemblance of the interlace ornament to the Book of Kells.

Many such wells survive in Ireland and in Scotland where they are known as clootie wells because pilgrims tie cloths to the trees about them as votive offerings—another survival from pagan times.

One of the most remarkable features of the impact of Christianity on Celtic traditions was the way in which, just as it gave a new sense and a new vividness to the individuality of men and women, so it gave a new vigour and a new definition to their art and literature. To take one example, that of the interlace ornament which we think of as typically Celtic: this form of ornamentation was unknown to the Celts before their contacts through Christian missionaries with the Mediterranean culture which first evolved it. Yet it was taken up in metalwork such as the Ardagh Chalice, manuscript illumination such as the Books of Kells and of Durrow, and in sculpture and architecture such as the many great crosses of Ireland, Wales, and Western Scotland as a delightful fulfilment of the ancient Celtic passion for swirling patterns, for divination in the eddies of waters, for riddles and visual puns. In Ireland, which was only brought fully under the influence of Western Roman Christianity by the reforms of the twelfth century accompanying the Anglo-Norman conquest, these artistic styles were practised far longer than anywhere else, being incorporated happily into the Romanesque influences which first appear in Cormac's Chapel on the Rock of Cashel. Again, the cultivation of literacy in the monasteries preserved rather than expunged the mythological heritage from the pagan past because for the first time the legends of the deities and heroes of Ireland were written down and recorded.

Unfortunately no such task was undertaken for the heritage of those strange people, the Picts, who nevertheless under the impact of Christianity turned to sculpture. Their crosses and stones, frequently carved with emblems such as mirrors and combs, have a life and a plasticity which is unequalled for their period.

One such stone stood, until removed to Edinburgh, on the Brough of Birsay on the Mainland of Orkney—a tidal island first settled by Culdees, Celtic monks working among the Picts. The island, chosen for its natural defences, was seized by the Vikings whose earls lived there in a long hall, traces of which may still be seen together with the remains of an apsidal church. Nearly every holy place mentioned in this chapter felt the hammer blows of the Vikings delivered from Scandinavia and from their base on Orkney. Lindisfarne and Whitby were destroyed only to be re-established hundreds of years later in the Middle Ages. A beach on Iona is still known as the Strand of the Monks where they were slaughtered by the Vikings. Coming at first to plunder and kill, the Vikings soon decided on conquest, seizing much of eastern Ireland, the Hebrides and the coasts of Scotland, and establishing their own kingdoms in the north and east of England. They made many martyrs, among them St Alphege, an Archbishop of Canterbury, taken prisoner, whom they murdered by pelting him with bones at the end of one of their feasts. Another of their victims in 869 was the young King of East Anglia, Edmund, whom they tried to force to abjure Christianity. They hung him in a tree, threw spears at him and then decapitated him. They hid his head in a wood at Eglesdene where, searching for him, the Saxons heard a voice calling them and found the head miraculously guarded by a wolf. His remains were later taken to Beodricsworth, soon to be renamed in his honour Bury St Edmunds, where in 1032 the Danish conqueror of England, King Canute, a recent convert to Christianity, was present at the consecration of his shrine. The abbey that grew up about the shrine was to be one of the greatest in England.

94 *Left* Westminster Abbey, London. The vault of the choir constructed by Henry III to rise above the high altar and the shrine, behind it, of Edward the Confessor.

95 *Above* Aberlemno, Tayside. A Pictish stone standing by the roadside, ornamented with a hunting scene and striking, but uninterpretable symbols. The other side of the stone is carved with a great cross.

The Vikings who settled in England, partly due to the prestige and civilized example of Alfred the Great and his successors, soon accepted Christianity. It was in Orkney that the old pagan ways held out longest, until the time of Earl Thorfinn in the middle of the eleventh century. It was his church that was mentioned above on the Brough of Birsay and it was one of his later successors as joint earl of the Orkneys, St Magnus, who, by his life and death, gave a new meaning to the Christianity of those islands. As a young man he was taken on an expedition to Anglesey where he refused to fight, staying on deck reading his psalter and replying when chided that he had no quarrel with the men they were fighting.[15] He was made earl jointly with a cousin who sought to dispose of him by asking him to a meeting on the small island of Egilsay. A church with a round tower built soon after his martyrdom stands close to the spot where, after praying all night, he was struck down by his cousin's cook. The cousin did not flourish because another relation, Rognvald, a gallant and charming poet, vowed revenge. He seized the earldom and engaged masons who had finished work on Durham cathedral to construct the magnificent cathedral at Kirkwall where, buried deep in facing piers of the choir, the bones of St Magnus and St Rognvald still rest.

St Magnus was martyred in 1117, sometime after the Norman Conquest of England had changed the pattern of life in much of these islands, but his story seems to belong to the earlier period. It is with another sainted ruler that we should close this chapter, the unearthly and immensely skilful Edward the Confessor, who at once by his reign restored the ancient royal line of Wessex after the English throne had been seized by Canute and his successors and brought that line to an end by his lack of issue—a lack attributable to his state of married chastity. He is chiefly remembered for his rebuilding of Westminster Abbey on a scale, as recent investigations have shown, greater than any contemporary church building in Normandy. The Abbey then stood on an island in the Thames. A week after its consecration Edward died and was buried in the Abbey where his bones still rest, leaving England to be ruled for nine months by Harold Godwinson who was killed at Hastings under the arrows of William the Conqueror's army. William maintained that he had been Edward the Confessor's choice as heir and did much to venerate his memory. The ancient blood of the Saxon kings lived on in Edward's relation Margaret who married Malcolm Canmore, King of Scotland, through whose issue it descends to our present royal family. William and his successors needed that association with the almost divine mystique of the Saxon royal line and Edward was venerated as a saint long before his canonization in 1161. The present position of his shrine on the raised chapel behind the high altar of Westminster Abbey is the work of Henry III who engaged the French architect Henri de Reyns to build the magnificent choir which rises above it. Eleven kings, queens and princesses lie in their tombs about the shrine of Edward with its holes into which sick pilgrims thrust their ailing parts for contact with his tomb so that they might be cured. Facing it is the coronation chair made for Edward I so that it might contain the Stone of Destiny which he had seized from the ancient coronation site of the Kings of Scotland at Scone. This stone was said in the Middle Ages to have been the pillow of Joseph at Bethel. It may in fact have once been the seat or pillow of St Columba on Iona. On that throne every crowned monarch has sat since the coronation of Edward II in 1307. Like the bare hill of Tara or the ruins of St Andrews beside the grey North Sea, the shrine of Edward is alive with the past and the destiny of a nation.

96 Kirkwall, Orkney. Part of the choir of the cathedral of St Magnus. Both St Magnus, the martyr who inspired its building, and St Rognvald who built it are buried in piers of the choir.

Chapter 6

Holy places of the Middle Ages: reformers, masons, and monks

The year after his great victory at Hastings, William the Conqueror founded the monastery later known as Battle Abbey in thanksgiving and also perhaps as an act of propitiation to the dead Harold of England. The high altar was placed on the spot where Harold fell. There the monks were bound to pray for the souls of both conquered and conqueror in perpetuity. William's companions in victory and their successors were to found or rebuild many similar institutions. These monasteries or their remains are the visible signs of the intense awareness of other worlds amongst all sections of the community in the Middle Ages—the awareness, at a time when death through disease, famine or violence was always close to hand, of worlds of damnation, purgation, and bliss awaiting souls about to depart this life, and for which a happier destination could be obtained through the prayers of the living and the intercession of the glorified dead.

William the Conqueror had invaded England with the blessing of the Pope. In general he worked very closely with the Church, then in the throes of the Reform movement. England was in fact conquered spiritually by the Reformers as it was in the political sense by the Normans. William the Conqueror deposed all but one of the Saxon bishops, the exception being the saintly Wulfstan of Worcester who, when told in Westminster Abbey to surrender his pastoral staff, laid it on the tomb of Edward the Confessor, saying he would give it up only to the man who had presented him with it. No one could move the staff until William conceded and confirmed Wulfstan in his bishopric. Wulfstan was to do much to reconcile the Anglo-Saxons to their lot by preaching that the Conquest was God's judgement on them for their past wickedness. By remaining Bishop at Worcester and with the help of Aethelwig, the Abbot of the neighbouring Evesham, Wulfstan managed to preserve much of value in the Anglo-Saxon monastic tradition. At Evesham Aethelwig met a Norman knight called Reinfrid who, in the course of the campaigns of the Conqueror in the north, had been disturbed by the ruins of St Hilda's Abbey at Whitby, which like most of the northern monasteries mentioned in the last chapter—Monkwearmouth, Jarrow, and Lindisfarne—had been left deserted since their sacking by the Vikings. Reinfrid became a monk under Aethelwig and made friends with Aldwin of Winchcombe who, inspired by reading Bede, wanted to travel to the north. Together Reinfrid and Aldwin with another monk travelled north and in ten years had re-established monastic communities at Whitby, Jarrow, and Monkwearmouth. They also founded the great Abbey of St Mary's at York whose ruins can now divert from his path the visitor on his way from the station to the Minster. Aldwin later became the first prior of the monastic community

set up to serve the cathedral of Durham.

In order to provide splendid settings for the celebration of the liturgy and to exalt their hierarchy in the eyes of the laity, the Reformers built cathedrals and churches of a scale and ambition unknown since the fall of the Roman Empire. Their model was the gigantic Abbey Church of Cluny, the Benedictine monastery in Burgundy which was the chief centre of the Reform movement which had also taken strong root in Normandy. Unusually by continental practice several of the Anglo-Saxon cathedrals had been run by monks instead of secular clergy or canons. As part of their reorganization of the English church they not only changed many of the sees to growing centres of population as when they moved the bishopric of Norfolk from Thetford and North Elmham to Norwich, but also made both new cathedrals, like Norwich, and older cathedrals, like Winchester, monastic foundations, confident that the monks would be more rigorous proponents and interpreters of the new ideas and practices than the old secular clergy. To carry out their ambitious building programmes the Norman prelates and reformers had to turn to secular help in the form of the mason architects and the craftsmen sculptors in whose numbers genius flowered, often anonymously, to an exceptional extent at this period.

With their skills the atmosphere of holiness was more and more developed through the creation of beauty. In smaller churches the attention of the sculptors was largely devoted to the door and its porch; it was here in the Middle Ages that marriages were celebrated and funeral services conducted and the door itself symbolized the entry into the higher worlds of the angels and of God and his saints in glory. Sometimes, as at Malmesbury, the door surrounds were carved both with the cycle of the months, depicting the round of life for the

97 *Above* St Mary's Abbey, York. One of the abbeys founded or refounded by Reinfrid and Aldwin in their revival of monasticism in the north-east after the Norman Conquest. Fountains Abbey was founded by monks who rejected the lax rule of this abbey.

98 *Right* Norwich. A chapel seen from the ambulatory of the choir of the cathedral, a new foundation of the Normans that exhibits the Romanesque style in its purest form.

largely rustic population, and with the signs of the zodiac whose symbols showed the action of higher celestial causes upon human affairs. Sometimes the tympanum above the door shows Christ with censing angels; sometimes a knight rides down a monster, piercing it with his lance, showing the triumph of good over evil. More often the vocabulary of ornament is more simple, more ancient in its origins, and more powerful. The surrounds of the doors are covered in series of chevron or zigzag patterns which are as old, in these islands at least, as the carvings at New Grange; often ferocious heads with beaks or teeth and tongues protruding to devour the band of stone beneath them recall the demon hounds of Anglo-Saxon folklore or the Fenris wolves of Nordic mythology. Thus they are at St Germans in Cornwall, the ancient see of the peninsula removed by the Normans to the alien jurisdiction of Exeter. To St Germans the masons took the blue Elvan stone from the quarries at Landrake to carve the beautiful door over which now the green pleurococcus grows, making a bright contrast with the colour of the stone. Sometimes the column shafts of the doors are twisted with tentacular vegetation in which men, animals, and centaurs writhe, as in the doors of Lincoln Cathedral or as at Kilpeck in Herefordshire which, though said to be the work either of Spanish craftsmen or else of artists strongly influenced by the Spanish Romanesque, depicts, more completely than any other building of the period I know of, the synthesis of older indigenous religious symbolism. Here Viking dragon heads stick out from high in the west wall and a series of figures and heads are carved in frieze under the eaves, the latter recalling the Celtic cult of the severed head. One of these figures is a Sheila-na-gig, an Irish phrase which politely disguises the depiction of a woman displaying her vulva or giving birth. Examples of this figure, which may

99 *Below left* Malmesbury, Wiltshire. The richly carved south porch of the abbey church with its bands of panels depicting the labours of the year, the signs of the zodiac and other devices, alternated with vegetative ornament and interlinked lozenges.

100 *Below right* Kilpeck, Herefordshire. The door to this small church which contains some of the most important sculpture of the early twelfth century. Celtic, Nordic, and older indigenous symbols are brought together here in a remarkable synthesis. Note the chevron device on the lintel with the tree of life in the tympanum.

well be a survival of the cult of the Great Goddess, are not unusual; there is one above the door on the inside of Cormac's Chapel on the Rock of Cashel. The contrast between the old and the new religions is shown most interestingly in two churches close to one another; on the font of Avebury church is carved a bishop piercing a serpent, the basic image of the Avebury circle and avenues; a few miles away at Winterbourne Monkton the font there has the Great Mother in the form of a Sheila-na-gig giving birth to the vegetation of the earth.[1]

Where the greater churches are concerned, it is the Roman influence that is most easily discerned at first. The form of early Christian churches derived from the Roman basilica, a secular type of building devised for administration and the courts; the rites of the Romans, involving sacrifices and fires as they did, required that they should be performed out of doors and the interiors of their temples, apart from holding the images of the gods, were not as important as the exteriors. Partly because of the early years of persecution and the need for privacy, Christian ritual was conducted indoors and this meant that, as populations grew, especially in towns or where there were much-frequented shrines, there was a need to provide ever greater areas of enclosed and weatherproofed space. At the time of the Norman Conquest there grew up a deliberate policy to match and outdo the Romans; the masons and architects who travelled as widely as did their clerical and noble patrons had plenty of opportunity to see great numbers of intact or largely preserved Roman buildings both in England and abroad. They adopted the round column forms of classical temple architecture and also the piers and arches of Roman aqueducts for the interiors of the great churches, sometimes using one form entirely, as with the columns of Gloucester and Tewkesbury, and sometimes alternating them as at

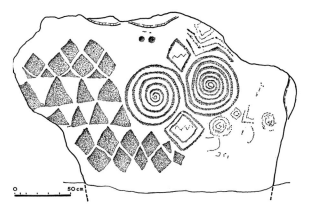

101 *Right* Lozenge, spiral and chevron patterns on a stone (K67) at New Grange, *c.* 3300 BC. Compare these with the patterns on the round piers of Durham (plate 115).

Durham. The effect of bringing indoors these forms originally designed for exteriors and of combining them according to non-classical rules of proportions is entirely un-Roman. The effect is Nordic, Celtic, elemental. At Gloucester, though no traces now remain, the gigantic columns were painted with patterns of vegetation in vivid greens and yellows. At Durham, not only did they paint the columns in red and black, but they carved the columns with the chevron, spiral, and lozenge patterns of the Great Goddess.

An unsubtle reader at this point might almost be forgiven for assuming that I am leading up to the assertion that the masons and sculptors of the eleventh and twelfth centuries were connivers at or supporters of the old religion. I am not. Rites and superstitions certainly survived, strongly enough felt for the medieval destruction at Avebury, for example, or for the death of William Rufus to be

102 *Left* Clonfert, Mayo.
The west door of the
cathedral (*c.* 1170) with its
gable ornamented with
human heads peering out
between triangles and
from the arches of the
arcade below. Eight orders
of jambs and seven orders
of arches surround the
door whose innermost
order is much later—
fifteenth-century.

103 *Above right*
Gloucester. The great
round piers of the nave,
once painted with
elaborate patterns. The
abbey church of Gloucester
became a cathedral at the
Reformation.

interpreted recently as the ritual murder of a king. The masons worked too closely with the clergy who were the chief enemies of the old religions for them to have such affiliations. What has to be understood first of all is that these masons were artists and therefore both interpreters and transcenders of their epoch. To enter the nave at Durham and to look at those columns and piers is to receive a violent aesthetic shock; they express at once the entry of the higher energies of eternity into the world of time and history and also the energy of their particular epoch in history. In the forty years, from 1093 to 1133, that was taken in the building of them and the great vaults they support, Jerusalem was taken for Christianity and north-western Europe had expanded to a point unsurpassed since the Celtic invasions of the fourth century BC. When a new spirit walks abroad, older spirits awake and become fellow companions on his journey. Just as in the revival and spread of the Arthurian legends at the same period, when legends, myths and symbols from the Celtic and pre-Celtic past were revived and transfigured in the renaissance of the ancient Bear god as Arthur the godly Christian prince, so the symbols of the Great Mother and the animal and vegetation imagery of remote antiquity which they absorbed with the milk, the spells, and the rhymes of their peasant mothers, reappeared in the dreams and waking visions of these artists, beseeching to be included and redeemed within blest and sacred Christian stones but uncompromisingly keeping their individuality.

Irish Romanesque, in its late flowering and in its transitional period, produced some of the loveliest work in the style. With its subtlety of interlace ornament, its lighthearted and fantastic monsters, and above all the purity of its line, examples of this style may be found up and down Ireland, often in ruined and roofless

churches such as the group at Kilmacduagh or built around with later constructions as with the great arch at Tuam. The finest of all to my mind is the work at Clonfert, originally the foundation of St Brendan the Navigator and now a cathedral of the Church of Ireland. Miles from anywhere and on the far side of the river Shannon from Clonmacnois, it contains in the wide splayed windows of the choir work of exceptional beauty, but more than that it possesses a door that could well make the visitor think he was about to find strange worlds beyond it. The best way to appreciate this door both from a practical and a spiritual point of view is to get down on your knees on the grass of the churchyard. The triangular gable is made up of reversed triangles with heads of saints and apostles poking out. These stand above an arcade which itself stands over the curving voussoirs of the door and the filigree carving of the capitals and the clusters of column shafts. If there is happiness in holiness this is the place to find evidence of it.

Shortly after this must have been built, Somerset masons brought to Ireland not only their skills but the Somerset stone they knew from building the first Gothic cathedral in Europe to employ the pointed arch throughout, that of Wells. With this stone they constructed the first cathedral of Dublin, Christ Church, of which only the north side of the nave remains as their original work. Some years before the first Cistercians, chief among the early patrons of the Gothic style, had arrived at Mellifont north of Dublin.

Before turning to the Cistercians and other religious orders we must look at one small monument of the Reform movement. This is the tiny chapel built by St Margaret of Scotland, now standing on a rampart of Edinburgh castle. She was descended from the Anglo-Saxon kings of Wessex and married Malcolm

104 *Above left* Wells, Somerset. Vaulting of the nave of the cathedral. The rebuilding of the cathedral from 1176 ensured that this was the first great church in Europe to adopt the pointed arch throughout. The rood stands on the strainer arch inserted in the fourteenth century to support the central tower.

105 *Right* St Andrews, Fife. The east end of the cathedral church which was served by Augustinian canons. Because of its possession of a relic of an apostle, St Andrews had the greatest reputation of all Scottish cathedrals and by the end of the Middle Ages had become the primatial see of Scotland.

Canmore, the Celtic monarch who united Scotland with the help of Norman adventurers. Used after the Reformation for many purposes including that of a gunpowder store, it is now re-established as a chapel.

The religious order most favoured by William the Conqueror and his sons was that of Cluny. The two most notable sites of Cluniac foundations are both in Norfolk, at Thetford and Castle Acre. All the new orders introduced in the twelfth century, the Premonstratensians and Victorines, the Tironensians, the Carthusians, the Augustinians, and the Cistercians were of foreign origin except for the order founded by St Gilbert of Sempringham and known as the Gilbertines. Between them they were to have a profound effect on the political and historical development, the landscape, and the agriculture of these islands. They were allowed a mere three hundred years in which to enter nearly every region, to raise their churches and their living and working quarters, and to establish around themselves new communities. Yet, though most of their sites are heaps of stones or at best roofless ruins, the very phrase 'a holy place' probably first evokes in people's minds an image such as that of the skeletal window tracery of Tintern letting through the sky and the tree-crowded cliffs of the Wye, or of an arch into a cloister, as at St Andrews, where only a few columns stand and flagstones lie in the grass where once there was a daily round of work and study. How have they made such an indelible impression upon our national consciousness? What is it in their remains and their surroundings that attracts us so strongly and arouses such deep and barely expressible emotions?

These are questions to which we will constantly refer, obliquely or directly in the short descriptions of some of these orders and their sites into which we now enter.

First we should consider the orders of regular canons, the Premonstratensians who came from Prémontré outside Laon, the Victorine canons who came from the learned and famous foundation of St Victoire near Paris, and most important of all the Augustinian canons who traced their names and origins to St Augustine of Hippo. They formed communities of priests or nuns who followed a rule less strict than that of the monks and who were allowed far more contact with the world outside. The Premonstratensians were particularly important in Scotland, founding among their notable houses the great Border house of Dryburgh and also reviving the holy site of St Ninian's white church at Whithorn.

The Augustinians equalled the Cistercians in the number of their houses and in their complement of members. In the reign of Henry I his queen founded their house of Holy Trinity in Aldgate and his jester Rahere founded for them St Bartholomew's, Smithfield, both in London. The great Romanesque church of St Bartholomew's survives next to the ancient hospital of the same name originally associated with its foundation, and Rahere rests in his splendid fifteenth-century tomb beside the high altar. Henry I also handed over to them what was to be their richest abbey, in Cirencester where they also built the splendid parish church for the townspeople. By 1350 they possessed over 200 priories in England alone. In Scotland Bishop Robert of St Andrews, with the agreement of David I, dispossessed the Celtic monks or Culdees at St Andrews in order to place the most sacred relics in Scotland in the care of the Austin canons, as they were also known. The Culdees were given another site, St Mary of the Rock. Bishop Robert had been prior of the Augustinian house at Scone and he built on the promontory of St Andrews the church dedicated to St Regulus or St Rule, the Syrian monk who according to legend had brought the bones of St Andrew to

106 Dryburgh, Borders. A view of the crossing showing the north transept of this famous Premonstratensian house. Sir Walter Scott is buried here.

107 *Top* Inchcolm, Firth of Forth. The Augustinian abbey of Inchcolm (the island of Columba) may be seen on the right arm of the island.

108 *Left* Jedburgh, Borders. A view of the south side of the nave. An Augustinian house, Jedburgh was founded in 1138 by David I.

Scotland in the fourth century AD. The tall tower of St Rule still stands outside the ruins of the cathedral which was begun by Bishop Arnold in 1160. It was planned to be the second longest cathedral of its time in Britain after Norwich, but a storm destroyed its west end in 1275 and in the rebuilding it was decided to shorten the nave by two of its bays. One remarkable feature of the site is that it still retains its monastic wall, nearly a mile long and enclosing an area of thirty acres. Within this precinct can be seen not only the ruins of the cathedral but also much of the layout of the cloister, the chapter-houses, and other buildings of the monastic community. The Augustinians were particularly close to the Scottish royal family: they also held the famous abbey of Holy Rood House at Edinburgh, the island monastery of Inchcolm in the Firth of Forth and another of the great Border abbeys, that of Jedburgh. St Andrews under Bishop Lamberton was a stronghold of resistance to the English in the Scottish War of Independence in the early fourteenth century, and the consecration of the cathedral in 1318 in the presence of Robert Bruce must have been a triumphal occasion, all the more because by that date the English claims and attacks had largely been defeated. This independence was to be confirmed, two years later, further up the coast at Arbroath. Here now stand the magnificent ruins of Arbroath Abbey, founded to commemorate Thomas à Becket by William the Lion in 1178. It was one of the few foundations in these islands of the order of monks from Tiron in Normandy. On 5 April 1320 the nobles of Scotland gathered here to assert the independence of Scotland in a document known as the Declaration of Arbroath.

Of the greater Augustinian houses in England, the churches of three have survived because at the Reformation one was already a cathedral, that of Carlisle, and two others, the abbey churches of Bristol and of St Frideswide's, Oxford, both became the cathedrals of new dioceses. It may be a result of the open nature of the Augustinian order and a shared delight in works of architecture that all three possess choirs of exceptional magnificence. Carlisle possesses what is generally regarded as the finest east window in the Decorated style, Oxford boasts the most splendid star vaults in the kingdom, while the choir of Bristol with its aisles has been described as the most important building of its time in Europe. Most Augustinian houses were not of this grandeur; I think in contrast of the small ruined buildings at Annaghdown beside Lough Corrib in the west of Ireland to which a group of Augustinian nuns came in the early twelfth century.

The richness of decoration of these great churches was wholly alien to the spirit of the founders of the Augustinians' chief rivals for popularity, wealth, and influence, the Cistercians.

The order was founded at Cîteaux in Burgundy in 1098 by monks who wanted to revive the purity and simplicity of early Benedictine monasticism. There is no stronger sign of a revolution impending in the future than a return to the primitive ideals and practices of the remote past. Under its second abbot, the Englishman Stephen Harding, the order found its new ideals and its organization which was far more constitutional and egalitarian than that of the older orders. In St Bernard of Clairvaux it found its greatest publicist and its greatest spiritual leader. He issued a call to the young men of Europe that, by the thousands, they accepted to go out to the wild places, renouncing wealth, luxury, ornament, and, through work and prayer, to make the wilderness flourish and their souls experience the heights of spiritual enlightenment. Their greatest effect in Europe as a whole was to develop the vast barren and

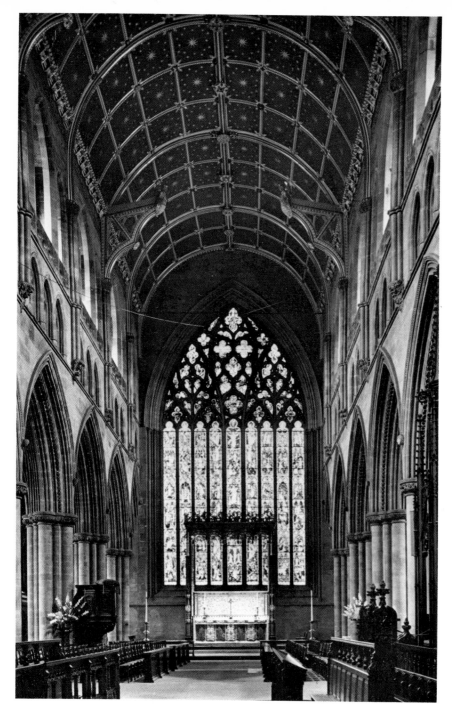

109 *Left* Carlisle. The choir of the cathedral looking towards the east window, one of the greatest masterpieces of the Decorated style. The capitals of the columns are carved with the labours of the year.

110 *Right* Oxford. The star vaults of the cathedral choir, formerly the Augustinian house of St Frideswide. These vaults were begun in 1478.

111 *Overleaf* Tintern Abbey, Gwent. The first and most famous Cistercian house in Wales, founded in 1131, Tintern is set in the incomparable landscape of the Wye valley.

112 *Page 126* Fountains Abbey, North Yorkshire. The cellarium in part of which the *conversi* or lay brothers of this Cistercian abbey had their frater or common-room.

unpopulated tracts of Germany, but in the British Isles they also brought great areas into cultivation or under pasture. Acting from the highest spiritual ideals, St Bernard gave a new direction to the release of energy already tapped by the Normans in the expansion of Europe and, though the abbeys, to which his letters winged with exhortations and spiritual and practical advice, are in ruins, much of the effect of his labours lasts.

The first Cistercian house in England was at Waverley in Surrey, founded in 1128. It was the founding of Rievaulx in Yorkshire in 1132 that gave the great impetus to the development of Cistercianism in these islands. This led shortly to the founding of Fountains Abbey, the story of which contains much in it that reveals the inner spirit of the Cistercian ideal.

Thirteen monks at the rich abbey of St Mary's York, including the prior of the

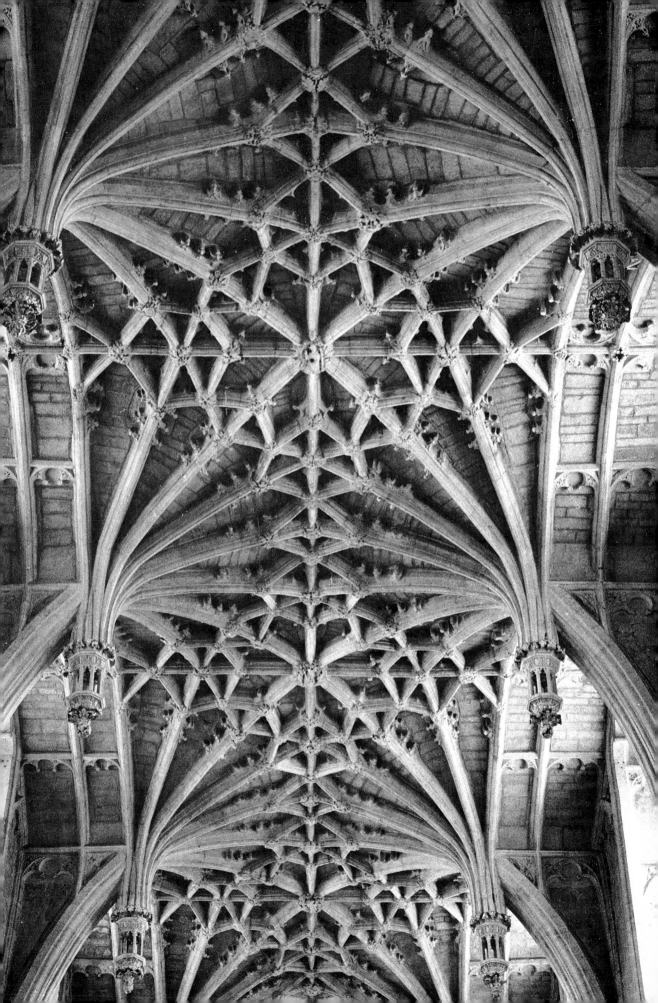

abbey, were disturbed by the laxity and the luxury of their life there under their elderly and kindly abbot Geoffrey, who could not at all understand their longing for a sterner and a more frugal discipline. They found the large meals provided difficult to resist and yet a constant reproof to their own weakness. Thurstan, the Archbishop of York, was sympathetic to these monks, but when he tried to intervene the abbot refused him entrance to the chapter-house. Thurstan laid the abbey under interdict and he, together with the monks, shut themselves up in the abbey church, afterwards escaping to Thurstan's palace where they were now under his protection. He took them with him to Ripon for Christmas 1132 and gave them a grant of land in Skeldale. They erected wooden huts under a great elm tree, where they lived in terrible hardship during the early days of the building of the abbey. The abundance of springs and streams in the neighbourhood gave the abbey its name of Fountains. The land was entirely uncultivated and the sufferings of the monks from cold and hunger were intense. In 1133, having elected Richard as their abbot, they wrote to St Bernard asking to be received into the Cistercian order. St Bernard not only agreed but sent one of the senior monks of Clairvaux to instruct them in the Cistercian rule. The fortunes of the abbey turned for the better in 1135 when the Dean of York resigned his benefice to join them as a monk, bringing with him money, land, and books. The community rapidly attracted so many recruits that in fifteen years it was able to send out ninety monks to found six new monasteries in England and one in Norway. All this was despite an attack made on Fountains by supporters of William Fitzherbert, Thurstan's successor as Archbishop of York, whom St Bernard and other Cistercians wanted deposed. The attackers wanted to murder the abbot but they overlooked him because he was lying prostrate in front of the altar.

Though most of the buildings at Fountains are roofless, including the abbey church, with its spectacular second transept at the east end forming a chapel of nine altars as at Durham, so much remains of the walls of the monastic complex that it is one of the finest sites for appreciating all the various sides of Cistercian life. Furthermore it is set in a valley of great beauty, superbly landscaped and wooded in the later eighteenth century when it was incorporated into the estate of Studley Royal. The disposition of the monastery buildings beside, and in some cases over, the river Skell reminds us of the Cistercians' ability in harnessing water power. As they created self-supporting communities, so they would use the water for driving corn-mills, bellows for furnaces and fulling mills for cloth, or for heating vats, as well as for disposing of waste and sewage downstream of these activities. It seems strange to say so but at no time in previous history had man made so much use of machines as in the twelfth century:[2] for the purposes of maintaining in wild and sequestered places large communities strong and healthy for prayer and labour the Cistercians were masters of this technology. One of the parts of Fountains that survives with its vaulting intact is the very long cellarium which forms part of the west range. This was the frater or common-room of the lay brothers or *conversi*. The Cistercians had opened the monastic life to illiterate peasants on a scale unheard of before: in place of saying offices which they could not read they were permitted to substitute their labour instead. Much of the early success of the Cistercians in founding their monasteries must have been owed to these *conversi*. In later days the supply dried up and the monks had to employ servants and labourers. Another important element in their success was the centralized organization of their farming.

113 *Left* Melrose Abbey, Borders. Aisle chapels of the nave. A Cistercian foundation from Rievaulx, Melrose suffered many times in the wars of the English with the Scots.

114 *Right* Sweetheart Abbey, Dumfries and Galloway. A view of the nave from the north aisle. Founded by Devorguilla Balliol in 1273, this Cistercian abbey took its name from the heart of its foundress's husband which was buried here with her when she died.

115 *Left* Durham. The interior of the nave showing the alternation of round and shafted piers. The lozenge and chevron patterns on the round piers are both designs of great antiquity, going back as far as the time of New Grange (see plate 101).

116 *Above* Kilmacduagh, Clare. The round tower and cathedral of this fascinating site on the edge of the Burren mountains.

117 *Overleaf* Mellifont, Louth. The first Cistercian house in Ireland, founded in 1142 by St Malachi with monks from Clairvaux. This view shows the ruins of the octagonal lavabo or washing place of the monks.

For the atmosphere of a Cistercian monastery in the heyday of their early founding there is no better source than Walter Daniel's life of the sainted Ailred of Rievaulx. The present abbey church of which the eastern portions remain as one of the most sublime creations of the Early English Gothic style is later than Ailred's time. The whole complex, nearly as complete as Fountains, was also the subject of eighteenth-century improvement when the landowner in 1758 constructed the Rievaulx terraces from which fine views of the ruins may be seen. Ailred was Abbot of Rievaulx from 1147 till his death in 1167. Born to a family of hereditary priests at Hexham, as a young man he gained the favour of King David I of Scotland. In 1134, on a mission to Archbishop Thurstan of York on behalf of the King, he called at Rievaulx. He set off for Scotland but turned back on the journey, returning to Rievaulx where he demanded and was granted admission. He wrote many works, the most popular of which was a book on Christian friendship which may have influenced Dante in the writing of *La Vita Nuova*. His personal austerity was extreme. He had built 'a small chamber of brick under the floor of the novice-house, like a little tank, into which water flowed from hidden rills. ... Ailred would enter this contrivance when he was alone and undisturbed, and immerse his whole body in the icy cold water and so quench the heat in himself of every vice'.[3] As for his effect on the fortunes of the abbey, Walter Daniel says: 'He doubled all things in it—monks, *conversi*, laymen, farms, lands and every kind of equipment; indeed he trebled the intensity of the monastic life and its charity. On feast days you might see the church crowded with the brethren like bees in a hive, unable to move forward because of the multitude, clustered together, rather, and compacted into one angelical body.'[4]

Among the daughter houses of Rievaulx was the greatest of the Scottish Border abbeys, Melrose, established at the request of David I, in the place where St Aidan had first founded a monastery. The remains there are the best in Scotland, though of the several other Scottish Cistercian houses mention must be made of Dundrennan, also founded from Rievaulx, and of Sweetheart Abbey in Galloway, so named because it was founded by Devorguilla Balliol who prized her husband so highly that after his death she carried his embalmed heart everywhere with her and arranged for it to be buried beside her in the abbey on her death in 1289. The Cistercians spread also in Wales, where among the remains of their work and sojourn there are the charmingly named abbeys of Strata Florida and Valle Crucis. The first of their foundations in Wales is also the most famous. This is Tintern, founded in 1131 beside the river Wye and, where its church is concerned, exceptionally complete.

The Cistercians also crossed to Ireland where their first house, at Mellifont, was founded with the blessing of St Malachi in 1142. Here, though little remains of the church, there survive a great gatehouse, the chapter-house, and most interestingly of all, the octagonal lavabo or washplace. My favourite among the Irish Cistercian monasteries I have seen is Corcomroe, hidden up in the wilderness of the Burren mountains. It was founded by Donal O'Brien in 1194. Fine carvings, unusual in a Cistercian church where such frivolities were generally banned, survive in the mouldings and capitals. Here kings of Thomond and princes of the Burren chose to be interred, holders of titles of little moment outside their small borders, magnificent lords to their small clans, men touched by the far-stretching civilizing influence of the Cistercian order. Of the other monastic orders introduced in the twelfth century the Carthusians, with their extreme demands of silence and isolation, did not attract many recruits or found many houses. The most complete to survive is at Mount Grace in Yorkshire, where the layout of the individual cells may be studied. Their greatest son in England was Hugh of Avalon, later known as Great St Hugh, the friend of Henry II who was forced to leave his cloister to become Bishop of Lincoln. The remains of his shrine stand in the angel choir of the cathedral he largely rebuilt after the Norman cathedral there was brought low by an earthquake.

If the twelfth century saw the expansion of monasticism and, especially among the Cistercians and the Gilbertines, the opening of doors to the humble and the illiterate who desired the monastic life, the thirteenth century was the time of the mendicant friars, most notably the Franciscans and the Dominicans, who by their preaching and their going out to the world transformed the ideals and the possibilities of the Christian life. They rapidly attracted recruits of great ability, probably drawing away from the monastic orders those who in earlier years would have become monks, and soon were supplying candidates for the highest offices in the Church. Remarkably little survives in England, Wales, and Scotland of their numerous convents and houses. This is because they largely settled in towns where, after the Reformation, the religious needs were fulfilled by already established parish churches and their buildings were therefore pulled down or turned to other purposes. Their greatest remaining visible achievement was the establishment of Oxford and Cambridge as internationally famous centres of learning, especially Oxford where the friars flourished under the protection of the learned Robert Grosseteste, Bishop of Lincoln. His enormous diocese then included Oxford. To see Franciscan buildings at their best one has to go to Ireland where there were few towns for them to settle in and where they chose to be close to tribal centres. The ruins of Timoleague, Quin, and Ross (or

118 *Page 134* Castle Acre, Norfolk. Romanesque arcades inside the west front of the Cluniac abbey church. There are extensive remains of this important foundation.

119 *Page 135* Bristol. The magnificent choir built by the Augustinian canons. Their church at the Reformation became the cathedral.

120 *Above* Lincoln. One of the angels that give the Angel Choir of the cathedral its name. Built by Simon of Thirsk between 1256 and 1280, the choir contained the shrine of Great St Hugh of Lincoln (Hugh of Avalon), the Carthusian bishop who began the rebuilding of the cathedral in the Gothic style from 1192 onwards.

Ross Erilly) Abbey are among the finest works of indigenous Irish Gothic architecture. Of a severity and subtlety that is profoundly moving, they are remarkably well preserved, apart from the usual feature of being roofless. At Ross Abbey, standing in a deserted plain on the shores of Lough Corrib, tradition says that mass was celebrated every day there, throughout all the troubles of Ireland since the Reformation well into the eighteenth century. At Quin the friars managed to keep some continuity going even longer: the last friar of the original foundation died there in 1820.

The impetus for new orders and new foundations was largely to die out by the fourteenth century. This coincided with a decline in the numbers seeking the monastic life. For the thirteenth century it has been calculated that out of a population of three million 20,000 were religious, male and female, in the various orders—one in every 150 of the population.[5] Rich benefactors preferred to found institutions of learning, as with Henry VI's foundations at Eton and King's College, Cambridge. Rievaulx, which could boast 141 monks in Ailred's time, had only 21 when Henry VIII's Commissioners dissolved it in 1538.

For all their decline in numbers, power, and esteem, the monks and nuns had worked great changes on the land, changes that have never been forgotten. Although throughout the British Isles the monasteries were dissolved or, in the case of Scotland, were put in the hands of secular Commendators who assumed ownership of their properties, the ruined buildings remained to keep the memory of the special lives that had once been lived there. For Catholics from these islands communities were established on the continent such as Douai or the community of Scottish Benedictines at Regensburg. Then, with the upheavals caused by the French Revolution and the Napoleonic Wars, these

and other communities found refuge in Britain. The revival of Catholicism in the nineteenth century led to the founding of many abbeys and monasteries, sometimes associated with schools, as with Downside and Ampleforth. Monasticism returned to the Church of England when Father Ignatius founded his Anglican Benedictine monastery at Capel-y-Fynn in the Black Mountains and there are now several Anglican orders, including the Benedictines at Nashdom, the Community of the Resurrection at Mirfield and the Friars at Cerne Abbas. In a few cases old monastic sites and their buildings have been taken over by members of their original communities, as with the Cistercians at Pluscarden in Scotland or the Carmelites at Aylesford in Kent. Some of the Irish monastic houses have been restored and are once again used for worship, as is the case with Holy Cross in Tipperary, originally Cistercian. The Iona Community of the Church of Scotland now maintains the cathedral of Iona and has incorporated the ruined living-quarters in new buildings. Without the power and the wealth of their medieval predecessors but inspired by the same ideals, the monks, nuns, and other members of these communities make a quiet and steady contribution to the learning, the crafts and the education of these islands, providing, above all, centres of stillness that every healthy society needs.

121 *Left* Rievaulx, North Yorkshire. A view from the north aisle of the thirteenth-century choir, looking towards the south transept.

122 *Above* Ross (or Ross Erilly) Abbey, Galway. The cloister of the Franciscan convent set in a lonely plain near Lough Corrib.

Chapter 7

Martyrs, builders, and pilgrims

If the monk, enclosed in the monastery where he lives all his life and dies, represents the principle of stability in medieval religious life, then the idea of life as a journey may be seen in the pilgrim who renounces everything familiar to him, wife, children, farm, animals, and walks off to seek a distant shrine where the burden of sin will be lifted from him and special grace will enlighten his soul. In seeking the shrine of his or her heart, the medieval pilgrim was following a pattern common throughout much of Europe and Asia: pious Hindus flocked to the holy places of India long before Christ was born; on their journey to Lhasa Tibetans would prostrate themselves their full length for every step they took; and in Islam the holy places of Mecca, Medina, and Jerusalem were then as now centres of devotion to which pilgrim routes threaded their way, from the Western Mediterranean to the high Pamirs.

The fact that Jerusalem is a holy place to both Christians and Moslems—as well as, of course, to the Jews—was the main cause of the first Crusade. The most demanding pilgrimage that could be undertaken came to be known as the Great Pilgrimage. For someone travelling from Western Europe it began by taking ship for Damietta in Egypt from one of the Italian ports and journeying across the Sinai desert to the monastery of St Catherine, then to Jerusalem, visiting the holy places associated with Christ and the Passion and then returning by way of Crete or Cyprus for the final stage of the pilgrimage, which was to go to Rome to visit the sites of martyrdom and the basilicas and to look upon the long-vanished relic of the Veronica, the image of Christ's face. A surprising number of people must have managed this extraordinary journey, given the numerous manuals and guide-books that survive from the Dark and Middle Ages on how to undertake it.[1] The next best pilgrimage was that to Rome, a journey also made as a matter of necessity by most bishops and abbots on their appointments. The appeal of St James of Compostela in Spanish Galicia was also very strong and there were as well numerous French shrines, most notably Chartres which contained not only a famous statue of the Black Virgin but also the tunic which the Virgin wore when giving birth to Christ.

The British Isles contained shrines of international renown but, apart from the Norse reverence for St Columba at Iona and St Magnus at Kirkwall, few attracted foreign pilgrims. The twelfth-century account of the Knight Owen's visit to St Patrick's Purgatory (see page 86) became widely known and was to inspire a trickle of doughty pilgrims to seek out Donegal. It was, however, not one of the ancient shrines that brought the pilgrims from all over the Christian world to England but the drama of the quarrel between Henry II and his former friend and chancellor, the Archbishop of Canterbury, Thomas à Becket, which

123 Canterbury, Kent. Henry Yevele's nave, one of the masterworks of the Perpendicular style, built between 1385 and 1405.

culminated in Becket's murder in his own cathedral and then moved to another
plane with the canonization of the martyr and the performance of numerous
miracles in his name or by his spiritual intervention.

The story of their quarrel and of Becket's death is full of contradictions and
mysteries which go deep into their equally complex and obstinate characters:
the charming and worldly-wise Becket, as Henry's chancellor, is one of his chief
aides in the establishment of order in an England ravaged by a period of
anarchy; the moment he is appointed Archbishop of Canterbury, he picks
quarrels with the king. Henry II, who more than any other monarch is
responsible for the founding of the English legal system, in a moment of fury
utters the words that license four murderous knights to kill the Archbishop. The
cause of the split between them was over whether a cleric in holy orders could,
and should, be tried in a civil court and be subject to the heavy penalties of the
time, as Henry required, or whether he could only be answerable to an
ecclesiastical court with its milder forms of correction, as Becket demanded.
From a modern point of view it is hard not to agree with Henry; but we must
make the effort to understand the attitudes of Becket and all those of his order
who had to fight so hard against the interference of the secular arm in the rule
and government of the Church. To them, a man who had received holy orders,
however lowly or minimal, however scandalous his personal life, was a being
henceforth, by nature of the rites of his ordination, different from his brothers
and sisters of the laity. He was sacramentally different and, owing allegiance to
another power, he should be judged by that power alone.

The quarrel came to a head at a meeting at Clarendon. Becket resisted the
king's demands and fled to France where he found refuge. In 1170 a partial

124 *Above* Canterbury. A
miracle performed by St
Thomas à Becket portrayed
in one of the thirteenth-
century stained-glass
windows.

125 *Right* Canterbury.
The view westwards of the
choir showing the high
altar and in the foreground
the *opus alexandrinum*
mosaic work on which the
shrine of St Thomas stood.

settlement was agreed between them and Thomas returned to his cathedral at Canterbury where he suspended the Archbishop of York for usurping his privileges in crowning Henry's son, the 'Young King', and excommunicated two bishops who had taken part in the ceremony. The news brought to Henry in Normandy drove him into his famous outburst when he challenged his courtiers to deliver him from this low-born priest. Four knights who were present hastened across the Channel to Canterbury where their intention was made known. Becket seemed hungry for martyrdom and deliberately taunted them in an interview in his palace. On the evening of 29 December 1170 the knights broke into the cathedral where they found him in the north transept and hacked him to death. After looting the palace they rode off, leaving the monks to attend to the Archbishop's body and prepare it for burial. To their astonishment the monks found under his robes a hairshirt seething with lice; they had had no idea that he practised such austerities. They also took care to gather up all traces of his blood.

The outcry in Europe against Henry was loud. Despite his first protestations of innocence he made public penances and in 1174 he came to Canterbury in order to show his grief and to be lashed by the bishops and monks present at Becket's tomb. Already by that time many miracles had been reported; a boy drowned in the Medway was restored to life, the blind saw, the lame walked, those suffering from hideous intestinal complaints were healed, either by prayers to St Thomas or by the application of water from the Martyr's Well into which his blood had been poured.

In the year of Henry II's penance at Canterbury a great fire destroyed the choir of the cathedral which had been built by Prior Conrad earlier in the century. So full were the coffers of the cathedral from the offerings given to the shrine of St Thomas that rebuilding could start almost immediately. The choice of architect and of the style of architecture for the new choir was of as great importance for the civilization and the development of these islands as the martyrdom of Becket was in its political and spiritual effects. The architect was the Frenchman William of Sens and the style was the Gothic, which had made its first appearance in France thirty years before at St-Denis, Chartres, and Sens where the first cathedral wholly in the new style was begun in about 1130. All the constructional elements—the ribbed vault, the pointed arch (in the vault itself) and the flying buttress—that were necessary for the development of the Gothic style had been brought together in the high vaults at Durham where the buttresses nevertheless are hidden by the aisle roofs. The Cistercians, always alive to technical improvements, had seized on the style for their later churches: Kirkstall outside Leeds, one of the earliest Cistercian abbeys to survive in great part, contains many incipient Gothic features of about 1150. It was the prestige of Canterbury as the primatial see of England and the shrine of a recent martyr that ensured that the Gothic would, in the various stages of its development, be the style of church architecture for the next four hundred years in the British Isles, giving the strength and grace of its line not only to the greater cathedral and abbey churches but to the humbler parish churches and to vernacular architecture. Gothic culture has, rightly in my view, been characterized as 'the purest and most intensive realization of the spirit contained in the New Testament'.[2] At last the churches would be built in a style that at once celebrated the humanity and expressed the spiritual aspirations of the saints whose bodies were laid to rest within their walls. In the sculpture of the Gothic artists there appeared a new visual presentation of the Christian idea of the worth of the individual soul, with an ever greater urge to transmit the personality of the saint or prophet portrayed; in their stained-glass windows, made possible by the wider openings in the church walls allowed by the high vaulting and flying buttresses, they employed sunlight and glass to depict the stories of the Old and New Testaments, the miracles of saints and the intervention of the divine into mundane life with a vividness and an immediacy that was far from the distant grandeur of Romanesque wall-painting. In the joy with which they observed the flowers and leaves of the meadow and the forest they expressed a new and original delight in the goodness of creation.

Gervase, a monk of Canterbury at the time, has left a description of how he and his fellows watched the progress of the new choir, of how they marvelled at the masons carving the capitals with chisels instead of axes, and of the tragedy of William of Sens' fall from the scaffolding and of his replacement by William the Englishman. The necessity of providing enough space behind the high altar for the intended resting-place of Becket's shrine dictated the unusual shape of the two Williams' work: unusual too is the chapel built at the far east end of the cathedral, known as the corona or Becket's crown because there the slice of bone cut from his skull was preserved. Glaziers worked on the windows which depict among other scenes the miracles of the saint; the floor on which the shrine was to rest was covered in the geometric mosaic known as *opus alexandrinum*. In 1220 the choir was finished and in a great ceremony in the presence of the young Henry III the body of the saint was transferred from the crypt to its new home. There in the course of time it became a treasury of gold and precious stones donated by kings, emperors, and nobles.

The approach to the high altar and the shrine was by a series of steps up from the old Norman nave. In the fourteenth century this was made more magnificent with the rebuilding of the nave by Henry Yevele who also designed new transepts and rebuilt the cloister. With its huge aisle windows flooding the interior with light and its immensely high vaulting Yevele's nave is one of the masterworks of the later Gothic in England. In time to give a signal of hope to the last generations of pilgrims to the shrine, the central tower known as Bell Harry was begun in 1496.

With the press of pilgrims coming to the shrine various routes or Pilgrims' Ways evolved, from Portsmouth or Southampton where many foreign pilgrims would disembark, from Sandwich which was the port for travellers from north-eastern Europe, from Farnham where pilgrims from the west and midlands could join those from Southampton and Winchester, and of course from London, which is the route taken by the pilgrims in Chaucer's *Canterbury Tales* down the Roman road of Watling Street.[3] The pilgrims would travel together for companionship, for safety, and out of a spirit of common devotion. Many other holy places provided rest and consolation for them on their journeys. Those coming from Portsmouth could worship, after his death in 1253, at the shrine of St Richard of Chichester, which became so popular that to accommodate the crowds in that small cathedral his bones had to be divided amongst three separate shrines. Those coming by way of Southampton would travel to Winchester where the shrine of St Swithin in the magnificent thirteenth-century retrochoir awaited them. The route from Farnham is marked by many churches that retain traces of provision for the pilgrims; at Chaldon they would have received a new sense of urgency for their journey when they contemplated the scenes of judgement that still strike horror into the modern visitor as he looks at the west wall. Nearer Canterbury they would be greeted by the

Carmelites at Aylesford. This order has in recent years returned to its old home and restored the Pilgrims' Hall. At the Cistercian monastery of Boxley they could see in amazement not only the statue of the child saint Rumbold, which could not be moved by the unchaste, but the miraculous crucifix whose figure of Christ rolled its eyes and moved its head in answer to the prayers offered before it. The route from London by way of Greenwich and Deptford led to Rochester where the tomb of the Scots pilgrim saint William of Perth, murdered just outside the town on his way to the Holy Land, attracted special veneration.

The pull of St Thomas's shrine was to people of all classes and all nations. Richard the Lion-Heart, Louis VII of France, the Latin Emperor of Byzantium and the Emperor Sigismund, and Henry VIII together with the Emperor Charles V all came there. In 1420 100,000 pilgrims visited the shrine—a large proportion of the population. Much of the attraction of Becket as a saint came, however, from the fact that he was a symbol of opposition to tyranny and central power. It was this that made Henry VIII so relentless in his attack on the shrine and on the crushing of the pilgrimage. The great space provided for the shrine, whose jewels and gold required 26 waggons for their transport to Henry's treasury at the Dissolution, now remains empty, but the pilgrims still come by the thousands and the tourists by the million to worship in and to admire one of the greatest works of art in the land.

The effect of the adoption of the Gothic at Canterbury was to spread throughout Britain and across the Irish Sea. Chichester acquired its early Gothic retrochoir. St Hugh of Avalon was soon rebuilding Lincoln in the new style. The shrine of St Cuthbert at Durham was surrounded by the Chapel of the Nine Altars. Many of the great Norman cathedrals and abbey churches acquired Gothic extensions as did Peterborough with the screen of its west front. The Norman cathedral of Old St Pauls, housing the shrine of the much beloved St Erkenwald, an Anglo-Saxon bishop of exceptional purity, was extended to become the largest cathedral in Christendom. Such was the awe in which royalty was held that the possession of the tomb of a monarch, even one as universally execrated as King John, could bring credit to the cathedral monastery of Worcester. When Edward II was brutally murdered at the orders of his wife Isabella and her lover in 1327 the abbot of Bristol refused to bury his bones; the more courageous and shrewder abbot of Gloucester accepted them, and the elaborate tomb erected there became the centre of a cult attracting great wealth to the abbey and allowing the reconstruction of the choir with its enormous east window. Not far away at Hereford a litigious thirteenth-century bishop, Thomas Cantilupe, was canonized shortly after his death, and there in the geometric style the north transept was constructed about his tomb whose base still stands guarded by figures of Knights Templar whose grand preceptor in England he had been. His intercession was thought to be efficacious on behalf of sick animals and Edward I would have any of his favourite hawks that were in ill-health sent to Hereford to be kept beside the tomb. Ely, which housed the shrine of St Etheldreda, acquired its famous octagon in the fourteenth century when the central Norman tower collapsed. Ambitious building programmes at shrines and churches continued right up to the Reformation.

Only one shrine equalled St Thomas à Becket's in international fame and that was Walsingham. Before describing that we must first look at three elsewhere in the British Isles that are important for the part they played in the development and maintenance of a national or regional consciousness, for their significance as shrines, and for the way in which they exhibit the growth of characteristic

126 Hereford. The north transept of the cathedral built in the Geometric style in the late thirteenth century to house the shrine of St Thomas Cantilupe. His tomb may be partly seen through the middle arch on the right.

national Gothic styles—they are in Wales, Scotland and Ireland respectively.

The first of these is St Davids, the chief and the finest of the Welsh cathedrals. It is built according to the Celtic preference for church sites, hidden in a valley, instead of following the English and continental liking for proud eminences. Said to be the fourth cathedral on this site since St David became bishop here in the sixth century, the present building is an anthology of all the styles of architecture from the Transitional style in the late twelfth century to the Tudor period, as well as the work carried out here by John Nash and Gilbert Scott in the last century. The interior of the nave, which was built under Bishop de Leia between 1180 and 1198, surprises first of all by its colour; the stone is a violet-coloured sandstone quarried locally. Though built after the choir at Canterbury, it is still strongly Romanesque in character except that the pointed arches of the triforium resemble those at Wells. The ceiling of the nave is of Irish oak, elaborately carved with pendants, constructed 1472–1504. Above the crossing rises the majestic and simple central tower. This crossing leads us to the thirteenth-century choir with the tomb of Henry VIII's Tudor grandfather lying before the high altar, to the north side of which is the shrine of St David. The base of the shrine contains openings into which the pilgrims could thrust their afflicted limbs and where they could leave their offerings. St David's remains are no longer here but are now preserved, together with those of his companion St Justinian, in a reliquary in a niche set into the wall dividing the high altar from the later chapel of the Holy Trinity, with its elegant fan vaulting built by Bishop Vaughan before 1522. What is remarkable about the whole impression of the cathedral is that its atmosphere is so much at one with its surroundings and with the original inspiration of its Celtic founder; many are the holy places in isolated surroundings that are ruins or, if still whole, are rarely the scenes of worship today. St Davids unites the charm of distance and solitude with the sense of a living and valued tradition. Its special sense of peace is felt most deeply in the Chapel of the Holy Trinity beside the bones of St David. I once observed its effect on the most boisterous four-year-old boy I am ever likely to meet. Sitting in that chapel, he suddenly became quiet, thrust all his fingers into his mouth as was his habit when reflecting, sat still for a while, removed his fingers and announced in the voice of a Pope proclaiming a Crusade, 'I won't be naughty any more!'

In the Middle Ages two pilgrimages to St Davids were considered the equal of one pilgrimage to Rome. Beside the cathedral are the remains of the fourteenth-century bishop's palace whose walls are ornamented in chequer pattern with the same violet stone of the nave. Here in the courtyard the pilgrims would be greeted and given shelter.

The shrine of our next saint, St Mungo, is set in very different surroundings. Amongst the gloom and decay of Glasgow stands Scotland's greatest surviving Gothic building, the cathedral of St Mungo. A contemporary of St Columba's in the sixth century, St Mungo (this form of his name is the diminutive of Kentigern, by which he is also known) was on his way from Culross when he came upon a holy man called Fergus who was at the point of death. After comforting Fergus through his last moments, Mungo had Fergus's body placed on a cart drawn by untamed oxen and told them to pull it as God directed. They brought the cart to the site of a cemetery that two hundred years earlier had been consecrated by St Ninian. Here Glasgow cathedral was to arise. Mungo buried Fergus in the place now occupied by the extension of the south transept called the Aisle of Car Fergus. The cathedral was founded by King David I in

127 St Davids, Dyfed. The cathedral seen from the gatehouse, with on the right the ruins of the Bishop's Palace.

1136. His building was destroyed by fire and was rebuilt in 1197. Little of this remains visible because in the thirteenth century Bishop de Bondington completed the crypt, choir, and the tower. The next two centuries saw the rebuilding of the nave, the completion of the spire and, under Archbishop Blacader (1483–1508), one of the most strikingly beautiful of the cathedral's features, the series of steps that lead up from the nave to the choir through the screen or pulpitum, going up sideways to the transepts and down on both sides to the crypt. These steps were necessary for processions and for controlling the flow of pilgrims. As the cathedral is built on the side of a hill the crypt is in fact a lower church rather than the subterranean room such a name implies. Above it the choir is a radiant interior lit by four lancets in the east window, below which stand the elegant columns of the retrochoir with its four altars. The capitals and

the triforium are richly carved with foliage and vegetation. Below in the crypt, however, the impression is very different: grouped about the tomb of St Mungo are four columns, set about themselves by rows of alternating thick and thin piers. East of the tomb was the Lady Chapel and four altars set below the altars in the retrochoir above. Here one feels most profoundly the power of the art that architects of the Gothic could attain, in submitting first to the requirements of their clerical patrons, to the needs of the pilgrims, and above all to the expression of the spirit of the long-dead, charming and compassionate man whose remains lie here. It is building of a quality that wakes you up; you walk amidst this mysterious space and the columns seem more alive than living people; the clusters of the columns and the fine ribs of the vaulting seem to speak the language of higher worlds of knowledge and emotion; and you issue out into Glasgow feeling that for all its sadness it owns the source of regeneration within its heart.

The comparative poverty of Ireland in the Middle Ages meant that few of her great churches could be built on the scale or even with the vaulting of the fully developed Gothic architecture of England and Scotland. The poor resources were rewarded with the development of a particularly pure and simple form of the Gothic of which the most characteristic feature is the east end of the church set with three tall thin lancets. Each time one comes across the three lancets at Kilkenny, at Kilmacduagh, and most perfectly at Killaloe the words of St Patrick's prayer come to mind, 'I bind myself today to a strong strength, to a calling on the Trinity. I believe in a Threeness with confession of a Oneness in the Creator of the World', so firmly does the design refer to the saint's teaching of the Three in One. This too is a feature of the Gothic cathedral of St Brigid at Kildare,

128 *Left* Glasgow. The shrine of St Mungo in the crypt or lower church of the cathedral. This thirteenth-century interior is one of the finest surviving works of the Gothic style in Scotland.

129 *Above* Kildare, Kildare. The thirteenth-century interior of the cathedral showing the crossing and the choir. This cathedral occupies the site of the monastery of St Brigid.

though it was heavily restored by George Edmund Street in the last century. The most notable exterior feature of the cathedral is that it is fortified with arched machicolation and parapets and even steps running up the gables to allow defenders to run to any part of the fabric walls that were under attack. This comes late in the history of Kildare, for once it was a centre of holiness, civilization, and learning.

Here in AD 470 St Brigid founded a monastery that was to be the equal of Glendalough, Ferns, and Clonmacnois. Her biographer Cogitosus, writing in the seventh century, describes the church as it was in his day, hung with linen, its panels painted, one door for the bishop, another for the abbess and her nuns, and crowns, one of gold, one of silver, hanging over the shrines of St Brigid and her first bishop St Conlaeth. Outside the cathedral stands a round tower of earlier date and also the foundations of St Brigid's fire-house, where a sacred fire was kept burning, for nineteen nights tended by the nuns and on the twentieth night by the saint herself. Brigid was born on 1st February, the old Irish Imbolc or first day of Spring, at Fauchart where a shrine is maintained in her honour. Her mother was a slave belonging to a druid whom Brigid converted to Christianity. One of the patron saints of Ireland, she is said to be buried in the same grave as St Patrick and St Columba at Downpatrick. The feeling of the Irish for her is recorded by Lady Gregory in this prayer said when the turf fire was covered up for the night:

I save this fire as Christ saved everyone; Brigid beneath it, the Son of Mary within it; let the three angels having most power in the court of grace be keeping this house and the people of this house and be sheltering them until the dawn of day.' For it is what Brigid had a mind for; lasting goodness that was not hidden; minding sheep and rising early; hospitality towards good men. It is she keeps everyone that is in straits and in dangers; it is she puts down sicknesses; it is she quiets the voice of the waves and the anger of the great sea. She is the queen of the south; she is the mother of the flocks; she is the Mary of the Gael.[4]

Part of the power of her name derived from the most ancient sources. She has the same name as the Irish goddess of poetry, daughter of the Dagda and sometimes described as the threefold goddess of poetry, smithywork, and healing. Many of the attributes of her ancient namesake were given to her by a natural process of association, and by their baptism in her a most powerful impetus was given to the reassertion of the feminine principle in religious thought and life.

The most notable example of this reassertion is in the increasing devotion to the Virgin shown from the early Middle Ages. The legend of the founding of Walsingham as the chief shrine of Our Lady is instinct with ancient associations. Walsingham is set in a part of Norfolk where the power of the Mother Goddess was very strong; a few miles to the south are the neolithic flint-mines of Grimes Graves where archaeologists found a propitiatory shrine on which the Goddess, carved as a heavily pregnant woman out of chalk, was surrounded by antler picks. In 1061 the lady of the manor of Little Walsingham, Richeldis de Faverches, had a vision of the Virgin Mary.[5] She was carried in the spirit to Nazareth and shown the house in which the Archangel Gabriel had appeared to Mary, the house of the Annunciation. She was told in her vision to note the dimensions of the house in order that an exact copy of it should be constructed at Walsingham and the vision was repeated three times to impress everything on her memory. She employed skilled joiners to construct the Holy House of wood but she did not know where it should be placed. Then it was noticed that the dew

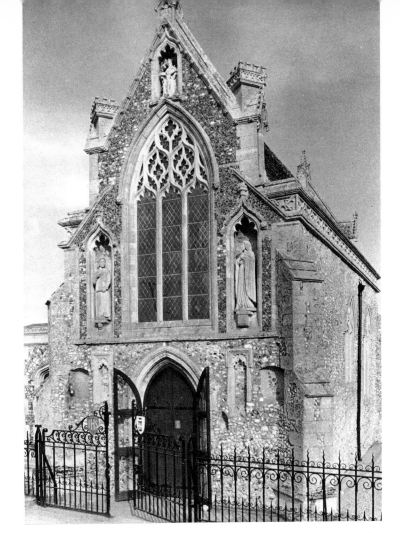

130 Houghton St Giles, Norfolk. The Slipper Chapel where pilgrims hung up their shoes to walk the remaining distance to the nearby shrine of Our Lady of Walsingham.

in a certain meadow left two rectangular spaces dry. Richeldis chose the one of these that was nearer two springs of water. When the joiners started to set up the building on this space, nothing went right for them. Richeldis prayed all night for guidance and in the morning they found the Holy House removed two hundred feet away and miraculously pieced together by the intervention of Our Lady and her angels during the night. In the course of time the Holy House and the stone church Richeldis had built about it came into the guardianship of a house of Augustinian canons, probably in 1169. Its attractions were further increased by a gift brought by a Crusader of a phial containing some of Mary's milk (this is in fact thought to have been white dust from the floor of a cave in Bethlehem known as the Cave of Our Lady's Milk) and by the presence of a wonderworking image of the Virgin.

The pilgrims came from many directions and as with the routes to Canterbury provision was made for them on the way. At King's Lynn the Red Mount Chapel was built for them in 1485. At Houghton St Giles a mile from Walsingham, for those coming on the route from London known as Walsingham Way, the pilgrims would come across a charming small chapel, known as the Slipper Chapel, for here they would hang up their shoes in order to walk the remaining part of the winding road to Walsingham. This chapel survives and is now a Roman Catholic church. It is at this point that the modern traveller begins to feel he is in a very special part of the country where the pure Norfolk light seems to have an extra radiance and the low wooded hills promise behind their tops a pleasure and a blessing. The pleasure is soon found in the charming small town of Walsingham, and the blessing in the ruins of the abbey and in the shrine where the cult of Mary has been revived. In the centre of the town is the priory

gatehouse leading into the park where all that remains of the Augustinians' church is the tall east end, two towers joined by the arch over the vanished east window. Beyond this lie the two healing springs once covered by a thatched building. To the north of the priory church lay the church containing the Holy House. This seems to have been destroyed completely at the Reformation, when the statue of Our Lady of Walsingham was taken to Smithfield to be burnt like a heretic together with other celebrated images of the Virgin. Henry VIII in his younger days had made the pilgrimage to Walsingham to pray for the health of an infant son by Catharine of Aragon. Like all his children by her except for Mary, the boy died—and the monks were expelled and the beautiful buildings became sad and lovely ruins. An Elizabethan poem laments the fate of Walsingham.

> Bitter, bitter, oh to behold the grass to grow,
> Where the walls of Walsingham so stately did show.
> Level, level, with the ground the towers do lie
> Which with their golden glittering tops pierced once to the sky.

This place was once called England's Nazareth and the whole land of England because of the special grace bestowed on Walsingham was known as the Dowry of Mary. The Milky Way came to be known as Walsingham Way partly because of the association with the relic of Our Lady's milk and partly because at night the galaxy shone over Walsingham as though guiding pilgrims on their way. The name seems evidence of a cosmic function attributed to the Virgin as the principle of love and femininity throughout the universe. Our Lady of Walsingham was particularly favourable to lovers and this appears in the most beautiful of the Walsingham poems:

> As you came from the holy land
> Of Walsingham,
> Met you not with my true love
> By the way as you came?

with its questions and answers and its splendid definition of true love,

> But true love is a durable fire,
> In the mind ever burning,
> Never sick, never old, never dead,
> From itself never turning.

Walsingham provides one of the most remarkable stories exemplifying the power of a holy place once desecrated to find regeneration. In 1921 a new vicar, the Rev. A. D. Hope Patten, was appointed to Little Walsingham. He had an image of the Virgin copied from an old seal showing the image of the original statue destroyed at Smithfield. This was placed in the parish church. By 1931 his efforts to re-establish Walsingham had succeeded to the extent that a special shrine was built incorporating a copy of the Holy House on ancient foundations that included a well. The image of Our Lady was translated there and as a result of Father Hope Patten's work, the shrine, undistinguished as architecture, adorned with statues and artefacts that are now out of fashion with puritans of all Christian sects, glows with the atmosphere of devotion, love and peacefulness that the gentle sceptic Erasmus records of the earlier shrine when, after praying to share the happy childhood of Christ and to grow in Him fed on the true milk of the Gospel, 'the holy Milk seemed to leap a little and the Eucharist shone somewhat brighter'.

131 Walsingham, Norfolk. The east end of the priory church, virtually all that remains of one of the greatest shrines of medieval England. The healing wells are in the distance.

Chapter 8

Dissolution and regeneration: the prospect from Primrose Hill

The Reformation of the sixteenth century swept away the active life of many of the holy places of the Middle Ages. The monks and nuns were expelled from their monasteries and convents and pensioned off, apart from those executed for active or suspected resistance to Henry VIII's designs. The shrines and sites of pilgrimage were largely destroyed, together with venerated images and relics. The lands and buildings of the abbeys passed first into Henry's possession and then into the hands of established and up-and-coming families. In the reign of Henry's son Edward VI, under the guidance of Archbishop Cranmer, an episcopal Protestantism with an English liturgy was first established as the state religion. The Catholic Queen Mary, Edward's sister and successor, could do little to re-establish the monasteries whose lands now belonged to families professing Catholicism on whom she depended for support, and her persecution of the Protestants did lasting damage to the Catholic cause. Her short reign was followed by the long reign of Queen Elizabeth I during which once again Protestantism was re-established and the religious life of the country was settled on the surviving part of the medieval heritage—the ten thousand-odd parish churches built in the Middle Ages, each of which looked to a cathedral of the same period, each of which through centuries of praise and prayer has intensified the atmosphere that makes a holy place.

The Reformation may be seen as the triumph of the vernacular over the old international Latin culture of Western Catholicism. Religion became a matter of the word rather than the image, of the sermon rather than the sacrament. This was so much the case in Scotland that where great churches such as Glasgow cathedral or St Giles, Edinburgh were retained as places of worship, they were divided up so as to ensure that every word of the minister could be heard. In England the new liturgy remained much closer to the old forms it replaced and so the churches required fewer changes to their interiors. Churches and college chapels continued to be built, at first in the late Perpendicular Tudor style of Gothic and then with the full introduction of Renaissance styles in forms borrowed from classical temples and basilicas. The Gothic revival of the last century, accompanied by the resurgence of Roman Catholicism and the rise of Anglo-Catholicism, saw the building of thousands more churches.

For four hundred years up to the recent changes in the liturgy the Anglican parish churches heard the celebration of Cranmer's Book of Common Prayer and the readings from the translations of the Bible later consolidated in the Authorized Version, a repetition of prayers and readings, noble in expression, that brought linguistic unity to England. The adoption by the Scots of English translations of the Bible, even if it thwarted the separate development of Lallans as a different cultural tradition, made the transition to the unity of the kingdoms probably much easier. The devisers of the new services had a long tradition of devotional literature in the vernacular to draw on. That Cranmer and the Bible translators had a language ready for the expression and translation of the complex Judaeo-Christian tradition in new forms is owed to the creation of English as a language of the intellect and the higher emotions by the authors of vernacular works among the monks, mystics and recluses of our holy places and by the poets and writers who drew their themes and inspirations from shrines, pilgrimages, visions and the telling of legends of saints and Arthurian heroes.

The monks, mystics, and recluses number amongst them the anonymous author of *The Cloud of Unknowing*, the turbulent visionary Margery Kempe, who wrote the first autobiography in English, and the gentle anchoress Julian of Norwich. The poets and writers include, most notably, Geoffrey Chaucer who set his greatest poem in the framework of a pilgrimage to Canterbury, William Langland whose *Piers Ploughman* arose from a vision on the Malvern Hills, the *Gawain* poet, and Sir Thomas Malory who gave new life to the Matter of Britain in his *Morte d'Arthur*. The holy place that most fully commemorates the English literary tradition is Poets' Corner in Westminster Abbey, where the names of those buried or remembered there make it a resting place of genius unrivalled in Europe except by Santa Croce in Florence. And just as Santa Croce lacks the greatest Italian poet, Dante, who is buried at Ravenna, so Poets' Corner lacks Shakespeare who lies by the altar of his parish church at Stratford-upon-Avon.

It is said that 360 million people speak English as their mother-tongue. The rôle of the holy places in the creation of the language and of its literature should be acknowledged, and because of this worldwide influence, they form part of a much greater heritage. Their continuing effect as an inspiration to our later literature is also noted in our remaining choice of holy places.

From the religious strife that followed the breach with Rome in the course of the sixteenth and seventeenth centuries, there remain many holy places, but they are sectarian holy places such as the sites of the burning of the Protestant martyrs at Smithfield and Oxford or of the hanging, drawing, and quartering of the Catholic martyrs at Tyburn. We can look with equal pity on the courtyard of St Andrews Castle, where the bishops sat comfortably on silken cushions to watch the burning of the early Scottish Protestants, and on the site of the beheading of Sir Thomas More in the Tower of London. We can mourn with an equal apportionment of grief the crushing to death of the Catholic Margaret Clitheroe at York and the burning on Guernsey of the Protestant Perotine Massey who gave birth at the stake and whose baby was immediately thrown into the flames with her. What is more, we can read the accounts of the trials and executions of the Jesuit missionaries as we can the description of the graveyards of the Covenanters with which Sir Walter Scott opens *Old Mortality*, aware as we do so that the beliefs and policies for which they died are wholly inimical to us, and yet be stirred to the depths of our beings. It seems a period a long way from Praed's Vicar:

> And when religious sects ran mad,
>   He held, in spite of all his learning,
> That if a man's belief is bad,
>   It will not be improved by burning.[1]

There was, however, a wider spirit at work to reconcile the differences, the spirit in which, for example, the Authorized Version of the Bible was translated in the Jerusalem Chamber of Westminster Abbey in a deliberate attempt to appeal to as wide a cross-section of beliefs as possible. This spirit of toleration is related to the mood of forgiveness and reconciliation which informs the last plays of Shakespeare. Oliver Cromwell was relentless to King Charles I and his followers who wished to impose one Church and one set of beliefs on the country, but the synagogue of Bevis Marks in the City of London remains as a sign of the spirit of toleration which he showed in welcoming the Jews banished from England since the reign of Edward I. It was under Cromwell too that there took place the gatherings of scientists and philosophers who were later to found the Royal Society, men who needed toleration for their task of observing nature and testing their observations by experiment.

For the educated classes the emotions that had been channelled through the monasteries and the pilgrimages went in two main directions. One of these was historical and patriotic. There was a new sense of the identity of England and later, after the joining with the Kingdom of Scotland under one monarch, of Great Britain, not just as a geographical entity but as a plot specially chosen by God for great deeds and heroic achievements. The supreme expression of this is in the speech of the dying John of Gaunt in Shakespeare's *Richard II*, but it appears variously in Spenser's mythical history of Britain in *The Faerie Queen*, in Michael Drayton's verse topography *Polyolbion* and in that great antiquarian work, Camden's *Britannia*. History was to become a potent political force. Just as the Cistercians had sought to re-establish the original and pure forms of monasticism and as the leaders of the Reformation claimed that they were returning to the practices of the primitive church, so the spokesmen of both sides during and before the Civil War drew on the various interpretations of the past furnished by antiquarians and legal historians. It is a curious feature of our history, closely linked to the regeneration of holy places, that beliefs, ideas, and myths long thought outworn suddenly reacquire meaning in the eyes of a new age. The most constant example of this is the Arthurian legend, which is re-interpreted in every century, but we can also point to the Catholic revival in Victorian times and to the immense cultural and political effect of the Celtic revival. Those who died in the 1916 rising in the Dublin Post Office are commemorated there, not by a Celtic cross but by a bronze statue of the death of Cuchulainn. A later visionary portrayal of the unity of Britain appears in Blake's prophetic poems when he sees the dawning of a new form of consciousness when sleeping Albion, the spiritual essence of Britain, will awake with the light of the Divine Imagination and be joined to his female emanation or counterpart, Jerusalem.

The other direction for channelling religious emotions was inward. 'My mind to me a kingdom is', said Sir Edward Dyer; the means of escape from political and religious strife and from the temptations of ambition was through the cultivation of the inner life which often found its expression through the art of poetry. It is because of their poetry that the places where these poets lived have gained their special associations: George Herbert at Bemerton outside Salisbury, Thomas Traherne reliving his childhood visions in great verse and prose at Hereford and Teddington, and Robert Herrick celebrating Christian rites and pagan customs with impartial ease in Devon. The place that contains in its seclusion much of the spirit of this inward-seeking urge is Little Gidding in Cambridgeshire, where one may still visit the church associated with the 'Protestant nunnery', the community centred on his family set up by Nicholas Ferrar in 1625 and which survived there for twenty years after Ferrar's death in 1637 in spite of its despoilment by the Parliamentarians in revenge for the family's giving shelter to the fugitive Charles I. Though the west front was rebuilt in 1714, Nicholas Ferrar's altar tomb still stands outside the church; within you may see many of the furnishings that were used in the days of the community. The place and its associations were forgotten until J. H. Shorthouse introduced it into his novel *John Inglesant* and T. S. Eliot gave its name a wider currency in his *Four Quartets*. It is indeed a place, as Eliot says, where:

> the communication
> Of the dead is tongued with fire beyond the language of the living.[2]

Little Gidding is a shrine of the Anglican tradition but there are many holy places connected with the tradition of dissent. Amongst the most powerful of these in their atmosphere are the old Quaker meeting-houses such as the one at Come-to-Good in Cornwall or the one at Jordans in Buckinghamshire. The meeting-house at Jordans stands amongst orchards close to a barn said to be built from the timbers of the *Mayflower* in which the Pilgrim Fathers sailed. It was built by William Penn, the founder of Pennsylvania, who lies in the graveyard outside. A simple building with transomed leaded windows, its interior sings with peacefulness and silence.

A different but deeply moving atmosphere attaches to many of the places associated with John Wesley and the founding of Methodism. I think particularly of the tiny chapel at Winchelsea where he preached his last sermon. Frequently forced to preach in out-of-the-way places where his meetings would not come up against the opposition of squires and parsons, he travelled the country endlessly, bringing comfort and help to communities like the Cornish

132 Little Gidding, Cambridgeshire. A view of the church and graveyard. Nicholas Ferrar's altar tomb, standing, as he directed, in front of the west door, can be seen centre right.

133 *Top* Come-to-Good, Cornwall. The interior of the early eighteenth-century Quaker meeting-house.

134 *Left* Jordans, Buckinghamshire. The Quaker meeting-house of 1688 associated with William Penn, the founder of Pennsylvania.

miners for whom the Established Church did nothing. Many of the sites where he preached are still used for open-air services, such as Gwennap Pit in Cornwall.

The Methodists may have been persecuted but they were not murdered for their beliefs. The squires and parsons had learned enough of toleration not to interfere with any man's beliefs so long as they did not contravene the game laws or the payment of tithes. While the Methodists carried on their conversions amongst the working population, thus making their faith the creed of the Industrial Revolution, the landed classes came under the influence of new fashions, including classical, druid, and gothick revivals, fashions which not only indicate the development of new attitudes to Nature but which mask deeper currents in the spirit of the times. This is shown most clearly in the rise of landscape gardening where, under the influence of Lord Burlington and William Kent, the enclosed garden disappeared so that in parklands and open vistas Nature was gently invited to approach the great houses. The *genius loci* of Roman religion, familiar to a class educated primarily on the Latin poets, was honoured once again with statues and with grottoes. Under the influence of William Stukeley, who regarded the megalithic monuments as evidence of a pure and primitive religion practised by the Druids, henge monuments and druidic bowers were constructed. This was not an inappropriate connexion because the gardeners of the eighteenth century, in works such as Stourhead, were carrying out the most extensive alterations of the landscape for philosophical and aesthetic reasons since the megalith builders of Wiltshire and the downs had carved the country in the likeness of the Great Goddess. The cult of Gothic ruins and the revival of forms of Gothic architecture portended a change in attitude to the past that was to reveal its full power only with the coming of Romanticism. Landowners fortunate enough to possess ancient ruins on their estates incorporated them as features of their grandiose landscaping scenes. Others had to have ruined abbeys and towers specially built. The ruins of Fountains were made the focal point of the landscaping of the estate of Studley Royal so that now one can approach them past a series of ponds, classical statues and temples embowered in plantations of trees. Similarly the Duncombe terraces with a Tuscan temple at one end and an Ionic temple at the other were constructed above Rievaulx so that views of the abbey ruins from above could be gained through gaps in the trees grown on the slopes of the terrace.

The love of the Gothic and the influence of ancient buildings and ruins soon had an influence on artists such as Turner and Girtin but also on the Romantic poets such as Coleridge and Wordsworth. Late in life Wordsworth translated the quotation from St Bernard that was once inscribed on the walls of Cistercian monasteries:

> Here Man more purely lives, less oft doth fall,
> More promptly rises, walks with stricter heed,
> More safely rests, dies happier, is freed
> Earlier from cleansing fires, and gains withal
> A brighter crown.[3]

The feeling that he shows here reflects the impressions cast on him in his childhood and early manhood by the medieval ruins of the Lakeland to which he refers in *The Prelude*, and many are the poems of his inspired by ancient holy places.

It seems right therefore to take as the last of our holy places one of Wordsworth's own dwellings. One can know and love Wordsworth's poems all one's life, but to visit Dove Cottage at Grasmere where he lived with his sister Dorothy is to bring a new dimension into one's understanding of his work— especially if one is armed with Dorothy's journal. Here is her entry for 27 March 1802:

> *Saturday.* A divine morning. At Breakfast Wm. wrote part of an ode. Mr Oliff sent the dung and Wm. went to work in the garden. We sate all day in the orchard.[4]

The simplicity of their little sitting-room in Dove Cottage is all of accord with her description of the day. The ode was the *Ode upon Intimations of Immortality*, the poem in which the shy freshets of eighteenth-century sensibility and feeling for nature become a torrent of Romantic passion, creating a new faith in childhood,

wonder, and nature, that was to give consolation and joy to millions in the horrors and degradation of nineteenth-century materialism and agnosticism.

From the story that has been told it is clear that a power of regeneration seems to attach to many holy places. This sequence of regeneration may be continuous over a long period and may link different cultures and religions, as with Cairnpapple Hill which spans the Neolithic period and the Bronze Age and Iron Ages, or discontinuous as in the cases of the northern monasteries such as Whitby, refounded in the early years of the Norman Conquest after being desolate for centuries. There is a functional explanation for their attracting resettlement or rebuilding; they were good places to settle in. That does not account for the regenerative power in memory, myth and the deeper impulses of religion which is often the cause of their refounding, as in the case of Walsingham, nor for the strength of their atmospheres. Indeed, it is possible that they are permeated with an objective force, imbued by the quality of the lives, art and thoughts of the men and women associated with them, which includes this power of regeneration. The power that once through belief in relics of holy men and women wrought miracles, now exerts itself through the atmosphere of landscapes, ruins, buildings, which are themselves gigantic relics of past holiness. Our ancestors knew how to name the force that resides in special places; they called it by the name of a god or tutelary spirit, the *genius loci*, the guardian angel. William Blake saw the essences of the holy sites of England as angels. We now have shy and borrowed appellations for the experience of the holy in a particular place: 'mana', 'the numinous', 'the spirit of place', 'good vibes', 'aura'; but that we have these words and phrases demonstrates the need to describe a common experience.

Returning to the line of thought developed in Chapter 1 we can then ask: 'How does this force, so much a part of common experience, affect us?' It can affect us at the removes of distance and of portrayal or transmission through a Turner painting, through the televising of a great royal or religious occasion as at Westminster Abbey or Canterbury, or through fine photographs such as those which accompany this text. Whether at such removes or whether experienced directly through visiting a holy place, it has the power to bring the dreaming, creative, reflective sides of our natures closer to the surface. This power is related to the inherited and acquired response we make to the archetypal forms and symbolism of landscape mentioned earlier, but it comes nearer to our awareness when focused on a holy place because it derives from the fact of spiritual transformation and creativity in our fellows, our brothers and sisters, our own kind. Thus this power can expand the heart and mind to an understanding of the deepest and most affecting emotions. To enter a landscape that has a holy place such as Rievaulx at its centre can be like walking or driving into an externalized dream: everything is at once surprising and familiar; there is an enchantment upon every lichenous growth and upon every blade of trodden grass. If, again, as at Rievaulx, it is a ruin that we are visiting, then the sense of strangeness is enhanced; we see through invisible walls vistas of columns and spaces we should never ordinarily see; our eye is taken up shafts to where the ribs of vaulting ought to spring and there as a vaster and more surprising roof is the sky; what seems a line of ominous still statues along the top of a high wall suddenly moves and takes scattered flight: it is the pigeons who are the permanent occupants now. A site such as Rievaulx is a constant evoker of our imaginative faculties, making the hidden artist in us recreate the forms in stone that were long ago carted away to make a barn or buttress a wall. The

135 Crummock Water, Cumbria. One of the Lakeland scenes that inspired William Wordsworth and through his poetry helped to create a new understanding of the spiritual power and peace to be found in the contemplation of Nature.

Tuatha de Danaan, the children of the Mother Goddess Dana, still live in Ireland; they have merely retreated into invisible hills of glass. So too, when we visit places 'where strange things had been done in the ancient ages', though we are there physically and no madder to our friends and relations than they ordinarily think us, we pass into invisible regions opened up to us by the atmosphere of the places working on our own dreaming and creative natures.

This discussion relates to the regenerative power of older holy places. But are we making new holy places now? When the missionaries, soldiers, administrators, and merchants took their English bibles off to foreign parts, in the course of making the British Empire, they set up a two-way traffic in ideas and religious influences. This led to the study and translation of the sacred works and texts of Hinduism, Buddhism, Zoroastrianism, and the Chinese philosophies as well as a more temperate understanding of Islamic civilization and literature. In the latter years of the last century the Theosophical Society was one of many movements that gave publicity to the spiritual wealth of these other civilizations. It helped to break down the rigid barriers of enclosed Western Christian thought and to introduce the thought of a universal religion, even if it was incapable of establishing it. The study of mysticism as the perennial philosophy also helped to reveal the experience that all religions had in common. The effect of two world wars and of the immigration of Eastern Christian people and of Moslems, Sikhs, Hindus and Buddhists has been to introduce into these islands more separate cults and religions than at any time since the Roman occupation. The monastic communities re-introduced in the last century, as was mentioned in Chapter 6, have now been increased by Orthodox monasteries and monasteries of various Buddhist traditions. It may be that these or the numerous temples, ashrams, and religious communities will produce men and women of the order of spiritual being that created the holy places of the past. It may also be that from some higher form of awareness there will be created a synthesis out of this vast range of belief and tradition, a synthesis that will include and make human the scientific attitude; that as one of its effects will bring about another fundamental change in our attitude to nature and our environment; and that this new faith will acquire shrines to mark its future spiritual triumphs, holy places that will resonate with new understanding.

We began with a hill in the West Country. Let me end with another hill that is now my habitual walk. This has many connexions with the revival of old cults, myths and religions and it may also be used for a viewpoint of the major religious currents in the present time. Its very name signifies the renewal of spring, because it is Primrose Hill, overlooking London to the Surrey Hills south of the Thames from its summit above Regent's Park. Formed of London clay of such a 'particularly unctuous, obstinate nature' that centuries of rain have failed to wash it away, Primrose Hill is a place of character: a personage of a hill; a green lump like a cranium whose indentations suggest thoughts of cantankerous wisdom. Given to Eton College as part of its endowment by Henry VI in 1449, it was purchased in the last century and made into one of the London parks. The modern orders of Druids who celebrate their rites there believe it to be a holy place of great antiquity, dating the revival of their ceremonies there back to 1717. Here in 1792 a body of London Welshmen, fired partly by radical ideas but more by Celtic patriotism, came together to celebrate a Gorsedd with elaborate ceremonial within a stone circle they set about them. What Iolo Morganwg and his friends started on Primrose Hill went home to Wales because their ritual was incorporated in the annual gatherings of the Eisteddfodau that have done so much to revive the love and knowledge of Welsh literature and music. The church on its northern slope was one of the centres of the revival of Catholicism in the Church of England in the last century. There is also an association with the revival of the Nordic myths and religion, because Wagner completed *Die Walküre* within sight of the hill at 84 Albert Terrace. An old tradition maintained that a barrow on its summit was the tomb of Boudicca; when excavated in 1894 it turned out to be much older, Bronze Age in date. A couplet given to that popular but invented prophetess Mother Shipton says that one day Primrose Hill will be the centre of London and that a cathedral will be built there.

You can look down from Primrose Hill south-eastwards to the site of

Londinium and think of King Llud who founded the city before the Romans came. The sight of a city as vast, as ancient, and as constantly renewed as London is awesome; still, in the record of humanity it is a comparatively recent phenomenon and it may make you reflect on its origins as a form of social organization which arose from the idea that the city was a god in whom the inhabitants participated as a right of citizenship and as the seal of their identity. Framed by taller modern office blocks rises the cosmic symbol of the dome of Wren's St Paul's on the site of the churches of Mellitus, the first bishop of London, and of his holy Anglo-Saxon successor St Erkenwald. Other office blocks still enable you to see the towers of Westminster Abbey where Edward the Confessor lies buried, and the Houses of Parliament. Nearer before you lies that monument of nineteenth-century scientific and exploratory endeavour, the London Zoo. This lies within the edge of Regent's Park laid out in the tradition of the eighteenth-century landscape gardeners and surrounded by terraces of houses whose columns and pediments derive from the architecture of Greek and Roman temples. Above the trees rise the spires of churches where they still sing Cowper's hymn that contains the lines:

> Where'er they seek thee thou art found
> And every place is hallowed ground.[5]

The glint of the dome of the Regent's Park mosque reminds you of the growing Islamic community of England. The effect of other Eastern religions may be visible about you as you come across people practising their Yoga postures or their Tai Chi movements. The hill raises you above the vast panorama of London; there, on a fine day, you will find the children playing and the lovers strolling, and the brightness of the weather may bring to mind the words that William Blake wrote, inspired by a vision on this very spot:

> 'What', it will be Question'd, 'When the Sun rises, do you not see a round disk of fire somewhat like a Guinea?' O no, no, I see an Innumerable company of the Heavenly host crying, 'Holy, Holy, Holy is the Lord God Almighty.'[6]

166

Notes

Chapter 1

1 There are very few discussions of atmosphere in relation to holiness but see Rudolf Otto, tr. Harvey (1923), where the discussion of the numinous frequently relates to places and buildings.
2 1 Corinthians 3, 16.
3 Carmichael (1960), p. 102.
4 Cooper's Hill, ll, 189–92.
5 See the examples under the entry 'Mountain' in Cirlot (1971), pp. 219–21.
6 From the sonnet beginning 'No worst, there is none'.
7 Carmichael (1960), p. 98.
8 This account draws on Whitley Stokes (1887) and Bieler (1979).
9 St John Gogarty (1938).

Chapter 2

1 For the importance of the cult of the Goddess in the Neolithic and Bronze Ages see the works by Campbell (1964), Dames (1976 & 1977), Gimbutas (1982), and Neumann (1955).
2 See Dames (1976), p. 159.
3 See Hodson ed. (1974) for studies of the place of astronomy in the ancient world.
4 See Dames (1977), pp. 176–81.
5 Tom Graves (1980), pp. 73–85.
6 Dames (1976), p. 54. The interpretation followed in describing the Avebury complex draws heavily on Mr Dames's writings.
7 Geoffrey of Monmouth, tr. Thorpe (1966), pp. 196–8.
8 Dames (1977), pp. 219–21.
9 This is the thesis of Euan Mackie (1977).
10 The Prelude, Bk. XIII, ll. 342–9.

Chapter 3

1 Lady Gregory (1970), pp. 337–54.
2 See Anderson (1975), pp. 141–6.
3 Julius Caesar, tr. Handford (1951), pp. 32–3.
4 Rees & Rees (1961), p. 162.
5 Rees & Rees (1961), p. 175.
6 Lady Gregory (1970 reprint), p. 141.
7 Tacitus, Annals XIV, tr. Grant (1977), p. 327.

Chapter 4

1 Tacitus, Annals XIV, 30.
2 Ibid.
3 See Rykwert (1976).
4 Geoffrey of Monmouth, tr. Thorpe (1966), p. 212.
5 See Green (1976), pp. 113–14 and references there.
6 Bede, tr. Sherley-Price (1955), p. 325.

7 See Watkins (revised edn. 1975), pp. 31–2.
8 Bede, tr. Sherley-Price (1955), p. 45.

Chapter 5

1 For an account of the Glastonbury legends see Ashe (1957).
2 This theory goes back to Dr Dee, the mathematician and astrologer of Elizabeth I. It was revived independently by Mrs Maltwood in the 1930s. See Pennick (1979), pp. 74–5.
3 See Ashe ed. (1968).
4 See Darrah (1981).
5 See Boswell (1908) and Patch (1970).
6 Jackson (1971), p. 280.
7 Samuel Johnson ed. Mary Lascelles (1971), A journey to the Western Islands of Scotland, New Haven & London, p. 148.
8 Jackson (1971), p. 279.
9 Bede, tr. Sherley-Price (1955), pp. 98–9.
10 Ibid. pp. 86–7.
11 Ibid. pp. 86–7.
12 The Poetic Edda tr. H. Adams Bellows (1923), New York, pp. 60–1.
13 Bede, tr. Sherley-Price (1955), p. 20.
14 See Hunt (1873).
15 Orkneyinga Saga (1973), pp. 54–5.

Chapter 6

1 Dames (1976), pp. 147–80.
2 See Gimpel (1979), pp. 15–40.
3 Daniel (1950), p. 25.
4 Ibid. p. 38.
5 See the figures in Butler & Given-Wilson (1979), pp. 72–4.

Chapter 7

1 See Demaray (1974) for numerous examples of these guides.
2 Frankl (1960), p. 234.
3 See the section on Canterbury and the pilgrimage routes in Adair (1978), pp. 35–71.
4 Lady Gregory (1973), p. 46.
5 The exact date of Richeldis's vision is both unknown and disputed. J. Dickinson places it much later, in the second quarter of the twelfth century. See Dickinson (1956), p. 7.

Chapter 8

1 Praed, The Vicar ll. 69–73.
2 Little Gidding ll. 50–1.
3 Ecclesiastical Sonnets, Pt. II no. 111.
4 Journal ed. Helen Darbishire (1955), p. 139.
5 Hymns ancient and modern no. 245.
6 Nonesuch edn., p. 652.

Bibliography

Adair, John (with photographs by Peter Chèze-Brown) (1978), *The Pilgrim's Way: shrines and saints in Britain and Ireland*. London

Anderson, J. R. L. & Godwin, Fay (1975), *The oldest road: an exploration of the Ridgeway*. London

Anderson, William, & Hicks, Clive (1978), *Cathedrals in Britain and Ireland*. London

Ashe, Geoffrey (1957), *King Arthur's Avalon: the story of Glastonbury*

Ashe, Geoffrey, ed. (1968), *The quest for Arthur's Britain*. London

Atkinson, R. J. C. (1960), *Stonehenge*. Harmondsworth

Auerbach, Erich, tr. R. Manheim (1965), *Literary Language and its public in later Latin antiquity and in the Middle Ages*. London

Bede, the Venerable, tr. Sherley-Price, Leo (1955), *A history of the English church and people*. Harmondsworth

Bieler, Ludwig, ed. & tr. (1979), *The Patrician texts in the Book of Armagh*. Dublin

Boswell, C. S. (1908), *An Irish precursor of Dante: a study on the vision of Heaven and Hell ascribed to the 8th century St Adamnan*. London

Butler, Lionel, & Given-Wilson, Chris (1979), *Medieval monasteries of Great Britain*. London

Caesar, Julius, tr. S. H. Handford (1951), *The Conquest of Gaul*. Harmondsworth

Campbell, Joseph (1960–8), *The Masks of God: Vol. I Primitive Mythology; Vol. II Oriental Mythology; Vol. III Occidental Mythology; Vol. IV Creative Mythology*. London

Carmichael, Alexander (1960), *The Sun dances: prayers and blessings from the Gaelic*. London

Cirlot, J. E., tr. Jack Sage (1971), *A dictionary of symbols*, 2nd edn. London

Dames, Michael (1976), *The Silbury Treasure: the Great Goddess rediscovered*. London

Dames, Michael (1977), *The Avebury Cycle*. London

Daniel, Walter, tr. F. M. Powicke (1950), *The life of Ailred of Rievaulx*. London

Darrah, John (1981), *The real Camelot: paganism and the Arthurian romances*. London

Demaray, John G. (1974), *The invention of Dante's Commedia*. New Haven & London

Dickinson, J. C. (1956), *The Shrine of Our Lady of Walsingham*. Cambridge

Eitel, E. J. (1979 reprint of 1873 edn.), *Feng Shui: the rudiments of natural science in China*. Bristol

Farrell, Robert T. (1978), *Bede and Anglo-Saxon England. BAR 46*. Oxford

Geoffrey of Monmouth, tr. Lewis Thorpe (1966), *The history of the Kings of Britain*. Harmondsworth

Gimbutas, Marija (1982 new edn.), *The Goddesses and Gods of Old Europe 6500–3500 BC: myths and cult images*. London

Gimpel, Jean (1977), *The medieval machine*. London

Gogarty, Oliver St John (1938), *I follow St Patrick*. London

Graves, Robert (1961), *The White Goddess: a historical grammar of poetic myth*. Amended enlarged edn. London

Graves, Tom (1980), *Needles of stone*. London

Green, Miranda J. (1976), *The religions of civilian Roman Britain. BAR 24*. Oxford

Gregory, Lady (1970 reprint), *Gods and fighting men*. Gerrards Cross

Gregory, Lady (1973 reprint), *The voyages of St Brendan the Navigator and stories of the saints of Ireland, forming a book of saints and wonders*. Gerrards Cross

Guardians of the Shrine of Our Lady of Walsingham (1978), *England's Nazareth: a history of the Holy Shrine of Our Lady of Walsingham*. Walsingham

Hodson, F. R., ed. (1974), *The place of astronomy in the ancient world: a joint symposium of the Royal Society and the British Academy* organized by Kendall, D. G., Piggott, S., King-Hele, D. G., and Edwards, I. E. S. Oxford

Hunt, Robert (1871), *Popular romances of the West of England, or the drolls, traditions, and superstitions of Old Cornwall*. 2nd edn. London

Jackson, Kenneth Hurlestone (1971), *A Celtic miscellany*. Revised edn. Harmondsworth

Knowles, Dom David (1966), *The monastic order in Britain: a history of its development from the times of St Dunstan to the Fourth Lateran Council 940–1216*. 2nd edn. Cambridge

Knowles, Dom David (1950 & 1955), *The religious orders in England*. 2 vols. Cambridge

Laing, Lloyd (1979), *Celtic Britain*. London

Laing, Lloyd & Jennifer (1980), *The origins of Britain*. London

Laing, Lloyd & Jennifer (1979), *A guide to the Dark Age remains in Britain*. London

MacKenzie, Donald A. (1926), *The migration of symbols*. London

Mackie, Euan (1977), *The megalith builders*. Oxford

Muir, Richard (1981), *Riddles in the British Landscape*. London

Neumann, Erich (1955), *The Great Mother*. London

The Orkneyinga Saga tr. Jon A. Hjaltalin & Gilbert Goudie, ed. Joseph Anderson (1973 reprint of 1873). Edinburgh

Otto, Rudolf, tr. J. W. Harvey (1923), *The Idea of the Holy*. Oxford

Patch, Howard Rollin (1970), *The other world*. New York

Pennick, Nigel (1979), *The ancient science of geomancy: man in harmony with the earth*. London

Piggott, Stuart (1968), *The druids*. London

Rees, Alwyn & Brinley (1961), *Celtic Heritage: ancient tradition in Ireland and Wales*. London

Rodwell, Warwick (1980), *Temples, churches and religion in Roman Britain*. *BAR* British series 77 (i & ii). Oxford

Rykwert, Joseph (1976), *The idea of a town: the anthropology of urban form in Rome, Italy, and the ancient world*. London

Squire, Charles (1912), *Celtic myth and legend, poetry and romance*. London

Stranks, C. J. (1973), *This sumptuous church: the story of Durham cathedral*. London

Stokes, Whitley (1887), *The Tripartite life of St Patrick with other documents relating to that saint*. Rolls series. 2 vols. London

Tacitus, tr. Michael Grant (1977 revised edn.), *The annals of imperial Rome*. Harmondsworth

Wacher, John (1979), *The coming of Rome*. London

Wainwright, Richard (1978), *A guide to the prehistoric remains in Britain*. Vol. I. London

Watkins, J. (1975), *The Alban Guide*. St Albans

Wilson, Roger J. A. (1980), *A guide to the Roman remains in Britain*. 2nd edn. London

Wood, John Edwin (1978), *Sun, moon, and standing stones*. Oxford

Gazetteer of holy places in the British Isles

Clive Hicks

Note: for convenience the names of the modern administrative counties are given here, whereas in the main text the traditional county names are sometimes used. All distances given are approximate. It is often necessary to walk part of the way to prehistoric sites.

West Country

Avebury, Wilts (beside A361, n. of A4, 7m.w. of Marlborough) One of the most important and impressive megalithic sites in Britain, Avebury comprises a great circular henge monument with major and minor stone circles, now also including the later village. The Kennet Avenue leads from Avebury to Overton Sanctuary. Close by are the associated sites of Silbury Hill, Windmill Hill and West Kennet Long Barrow.

Bath, Avon The Roman Aquae Sulis, Bath was established early in the Roman occupation as a convalescent centre at the hot springs sacred to the Celtic goddess Sul. The Great Bath and other remains, including those of the temple of Sul-Minerva, are to be seen at the Museum and Pump Room.

Bemerton, Wilts (1m.w. of Salisbury) Here George Herbert, the great Anglican religious poet, was parson.

Bristol Cathedral, Avon (on College Green) St Augustine's Abbey was one of the two Augustinian abbey churches to survive the Reformation by being converted into cathedrals. The choir is one of the most original examples of Gothic creativity of the Decorated period.

Burrow Mump, Somerset (beside A361, 9m.n.-e. of Taunton) A natural hill dominating miles of marshy land, it is crowned by the remains of a medieval church of St Michael, a dedication usual in hilltop churches. It lies close to a direct line between two other churches of similar dedication, on St Michael's Mount and on Glastonbury Tor.

Cadbury Castle, Somerset (beside South Cadbury village, just s. of A303, 7m.w. of Wincanton) Cadbury is an Iron Age hillfort, but the site may have been occupied as early as 2500 BC, and was used until as late as the 11th century AD. It is from its use in the 6th and 7th centuries that its traditional association with Arthur originates, for Cadbury has long been reputed to be his Camelot.

Cerne Giant, Dorset (immediately n. of Cerne Abbas; visible from A352, 7m.n. of Dorchester) A turf-cut figure bearing a club, he is 180 ft tall, and was probably a fertility figure, although he has also been identified as Hercules. Childless couples still visit the giant.

Come-to-Good, Cornwall (1m.e. of Carnon Downs and A39, 3m.s.-w. of Truro) The delightful Quaker meeting-house here was built in 1703; it is thatched and furnished with simple wooden fittings and is imbued with an atmosphere of deep tranquillity.

Corfe Castle, Dorset (A351 between Wareham and Swanage) At Corfe the young King Edward was stabbed by his stepmother in 979, and the church is dedicated to St Edward King and Martyr. The castle occupies a rise controlling a gap in the Purbeck hills, and is among the most elegant and picturesque in Britain.

Dozmary Pool, Cornwall (2m.s. of Bolventor on A30 between Launceston and Bodmin) This sinister lake, reputedly bottomless, is the legendary resting-place of Arthur's sword Excalibur.

Glastonbury, Somerset (A39/A361) A La Tène period lake village site, the remains of the abbey, Glastonbury Tor and the Chalice Well with their early Christian and Arthurian associations make Glastonbury a contender for first place among the holy sites of Britain. It retains today a strong atmosphere, and is a source of spiritual refreshment to people of many different backgrounds.

Gwennap Pit, Cornwall (3m.e. of Redruth, n. of A393, on unclassified road) A site sacred to Methodism, for here Wesley preached to 20,000 people. It is still used for services; its originally craggy sides have now been neatly terraced and turfed.

Knowlton, Dorset (nr B3078, 7m.n. of Wimborne Minster) Many churches are built on sites sacred to earlier religions, but few places show this more clearly than Knowlton, where the medieval church, now in ruins, stands within a prehistoric henge monument.

Malmesbury, Wilts (A429, 5m.n. of M4) The abbey library was for many years under the care of William of Malmesbury, the 12th-century historian. All that remains of the abbey church is the truncated eastern parts of the nave and a fragment of the west front, but it is of fine quality, and has a quite splendid south door and porch.

Merrivale, Devon (just s. of B3357, 4m.e. of Tavistock) One of the most accessible of the Dartmoor alignments of standing stones, Merrivale includes rows, a circle, burial cists and outliers.

Merry Maidens, Cornwall (beside B3315, 5m.s.-w. of Penzance) A very complete stone circle of moderate size, which may be seen under the quickly changing conditions of light and atmosphere to which the locality is subject.

Old Sarum, Wilts (beside A345, 2m.n. of Salisbury) This was first a prehistoric hillfort, then a Roman town at the junction of important roads, and finally a medieval cathedral town dominated by a castle. Its decline began when the see was removed in the 13th century. By the 16th century it was in ruins, so that now the castle mound overlooks the empty area of the hillfort, the cathedral's position marked only in outline.

Overton Sanctuary, Wilts (see **Avebury**) The Sanctuary now shows only the concrete stumps marking the concentric circles of post-holes which held the wooden uprights of a large structure, probably roofed.

Roche, Cornwall (B3274, s. of A30 8m.s.-w. of Bodmin) Set high on an unlikely-looking outcrop of granite is a chapel built in 1409 and again dedicated to St Michael. The chapel and the priest's room below are built of granite blocks, impressive evidence of labour.

St Michael's Mount, Cornwall (tidal island 4m.e. of Penzance, beside A394) The home of Celtic saints, and, without much doubt, of earlier holy men of prehistory. Tales tell of a visit by St Michael the Archangel. In later times the island became a monastery, but it has been in secular hands since the Reformation.

Scilly, Isles of, off Cornwall (boat – 3 hrs – or helicopter – 20 mins – from Penzance to St Mary's) The great number of prehistoric tombs on these outstandingly beautiful islands proclaims the special regard in which they were held, so that they may be the origin of the western 'Isles of the Blest', which fired the imagination of much later times. Sailing between or walking on them, looking at the ever-changing seascape flecked with islands on all sides, is a most exhilarating experience.

Scorhill, Devon (1m.s.-w. of Gidleigh, nr Chagford which is w. of A382 n. of Moretonhampstead) One of the best of the Dartmoor stone circles, and relatively accessible. It is beautifully sited on open moorland near two streams and is not far from Shovel Down.

Shovel Down, Devon (less than 1 m.s. of **Scorhill** – see above) The stones on Shovel Down are aligned in several double and single rows on either side of a ridge, the majority being on the north, leading in the general direction of Scorhill. The fall of the hillside permits a comprehensive view over lovely countryside.

Silbury Hill, Wilts (see **Avebury**; beside A4 just e. of A361) The largest man-made mound in Europe from the prehistoric period. It is based partly on a natural spur, and has been widely assumed to be a burial ground, but nothing has been found despite extensive searches. Recently it has been suggested that it was built as a symbol of the Great Goddess, the Neolithic deification of the female principle in the universe.

Stonehenge, Wilts (just n. of A303, 2 m.w. of Amesbury) The immense fame of Stonehenge has given it so grand an image that many people find it smaller than they expected. Visitors are no longer allowed access to the stones except on certain days, but this has the advantage of allowing them to be seen unencumbered.

Tintagel, Cornwall (off B3263, n.-w. of Camelford on A39) On a spectacular headland projecting from the cliffs of the north Cornish coast are the remains of a medieval castle and a Celtic monastery, as well as signs of earlier occupation. Tintagel is of course mainly famous for its Arthurian associations.

Wells Cathedral, Somerset One of the finest of English cathedrals. Like many others it is made up of disparate elements, all of the highest quality: nave and transepts, choir, Lady Chapel, chapter-house with its steps and the famous west front with its splendid sculptures.

West Kennet Long Barrow, Wilts (see **Avebury**; s. of A4) One of the most impressive burial chambers in England, with a large passage and five chambers, all built of very large megaliths filled in with dry-stone walling.

Windmill Hill, Wilts (1 m.n.-w. of **Avebury**) The hill was occupied in the 4th millennium BC, and is crowned by a causewayed camp, outlined by three concentric ditches with irregular gaps. Although the camp is not impressive on the ground, it is worth a visit for the atmosphere of the place, and the wide views.

Woodhenge, Wilts (just w. of A345, 1 m.n. of Amesbury) Probably a part of the Durrington Walls complex; concrete posts mark the positions of the wooden uprights of a circular structure, of which there were two more at Durrington Walls, now beneath the road.

Northern England

Bewcastle, Cumbria (20 m.n.-e. of Carlisle, mainly by unclassified roads) In the churchyard stands a magnificent high cross adorned with sculptured reliefs, vine scrolls and runic inscriptions, the best of the surviving monuments in England of the Anglian art of the 7th and 8th centuries.

Carlisle, Cumbria A Roman settlement even before Hadrian's Wall was built, it was later, for centuries, a focus for Anglo-Scottish warfare. Henry I founded here a church of Augustinian Canons, and soon after, in 1133, made it a bishopric. The choir of the cathedral is one of the great works of the Augustinians in the Decorated style.

Carrawburgh, Northumberland (beside B6318, 5 m.w. of Chollerford) The Roman Procolitia on Hadrian's Wall. The remains include a temple dedicated to Mithras and, nearby, the sacred spring of the Celtic nymph Coventina.

Castlerigg, Cumbria (1½ m.e. of Keswick on unclassified road) One of the most beautiful of English stone circles, impressively surrounded by the Lakeland mountains.

Durham Cathedral, Co. Durham The first church here was built to house the remains of three saints, Cuthbert, Oswald, and Aidan, by monks fleeing from the Vikings. The later cathedral occupies the same site, dominating a loop in the River Wear, Durham Cathedral is the crown of Romanesque architecture.

Fountains Abbey, North Yorkshire (s. of B6265, 5 m.s.-w. of Ripon) Founded in 1132 by 13 monks of York seeking a more austere setting for their spirituality. In the following year they were accepted into the Cistercian order. In its layout Fountains is typical of a medieval monastery, but more than that, it is architecturally rich and most beautifully located.

Grasmere, Cumbria (w. of A591, 7 m.n. of Windermere) Landscape was not always regarded as worthy of note, and we see it today through eyes opened by poets such as Wordsworth, who lived at Dove Cottage in Grasmere village. The essential character of Grasmere and nearby Rydal Water shows those romantic qualities which now find so ready a response in the visitor.

Hexham, Northumberland (A69/A695) The first church at Hexham was built by St Wilfred in c.675–680, and of this period there remain the crypt and his chair, which stands now in the wonderful Early English choir.

Jarrow, Tyne and Wear (on s. bank of R. Tyne, just w. of A1) Jarrow owes its fame to the historian Bede. The monastery was founded in 684 by Benedict Biscop, and part of his church as well as other fragments remain.

Kirkstall Abbey, West Yorkshire (A65, 4 m.n.-w. of Leeds city centre) One of the oldest remaining Cistercian abbey churches, clearly demonstrating that this order was one of the first to bring the Gothic style to Britain. The ruins are comprehensive, the church in particular being complete.

Lindisfarne (Holy Island), Northumberland (tidal island off A1 8 m.s.-e. of Berwick-upon-Tweed) Here are the ruins of the medieval monastery rebuilt on the site of that founded by St Aidan in 635. The island became a force in early Christianity in England, and it retains still a deeply regenerative quality.

Long Meg and her Daughters, Cumbria (2 m.n. of A686 nr Little Salkeld, 5 m.n.-e. of Penrith) This is reputedly the largest stone circle in England. Long Meg is a tall outlier; her daughters are the lower, rounder stones of the circle itself.

Monkwearmouth, Tyne and Wear (just n. of Sunderland town centre) The tower of an Anglo-Saxon church survives, surrounded by the 20th century. The church was closely associated with the holy men of Jarrow. In the entrance there is some extremely expressive carving.

Mount Grace Priory, North Yorkshire (just e. of A19, 11 m.n. of Thirsk) Beautifully situated, this is the best-preserved house of the Carthusians in England, and shows quite clearly the individual cells of the monks.

Rievaulx Abbey, North Yorkshire (w. of B1257, 2 m.n.-w. of Helmsley) The abbey blossomed under the influence and work of Ailred in the 12th century, but the buildings are later and, by Cistercian standards, exceptionally rich in architectural detail. In its setting, in its buildings and in its very atmosphere Rievaulx is extraordinarily beautiful.

Swinside, Cumbria (3 m.w. of Broughton-in-Furness on A595, n. on unclassified road, and along a farm road on private land) Little known, but one of the best English stone circles, complete and beautifully sited.

Whitby Abbey, North Yorkshire (A171, on coast) The abbey is located on high cliffs south of the town, a picturesque ruin in a magnificent setting.

York, North Yorkshire York was first a Roman fortress and later the military capital of Britain, and parts of the walls are Roman. Extensive remains from the post-Roman and early medieval period have recently been excavated. Central among the attractions of this fine city is the Minster, a great Gothic church of exceptional richness.

Eastern England

Bury St Edmunds, Suffolk   The town takes its name from Edmund, king of East Anglia, martyred by the Vikings in 869. His shrine was consecrated in 1032, and a great abbey built around it; little remains other than the gatehouses. There are two other notable churches, those of St James (the cathedral) and St Mary.

Castle Acre Priory, Norfolk (w. of A1065, 4m.n. of Swaffham)   One of the most important of the Cluniac monastic foundations. The abbey ruins are extensive and attractive, with an important arcaded façade and a well-preserved prior's house.

Colchester, Essex   Formerly Camulodunum, capital of the Trinovantes, the principal opponents of the Romans in Britain, it was seized by Claudius early in his campaign. A splendid classical temple was built here and dedicated to the Emperor. Its podium became the base for the Norman castle, which is now the museum.

Ely, Cambs (A10, 16m.n. of Cambridge)   The monastery at Ely was founded in 673 by St Etheldreda. It was destroyed by the Danes in 870, and the present building was started in 1083. The cathedral has a noble Norman nave, an early Gothic choir, a richly decorated Lady Chapel and the famous octagonal lantern above the crossing.

Lincoln, Lincs   The cathedral has a good claim to be the richest and fullest work of Gothic architecture in Britain, built as it was when the Gothic style in this country was reaching its greatest heights of expressive spirituality. Great St Hugh, bishop of Lincoln, began the rebuilding in its present form.

Little Gidding, Cambs (15m.s. of Peterborough, e. of B660 off A1)   The tranquillity of this remote churchyard calls to mind the life and work of Nicholas Ferrar who established a community here in 1625, but today perhaps more people are drawn by the transforming quality of T. S. Eliot's *Four Quartets*.

Norwich, Norfolk   The cathedral was built as a result of the removal of the see from North Elmham in 1091, and it is one of the great Norman churches of England. It also has splendid Perpendicular vaults to the nave and the choir, and cloisters rich in carved bosses.

Walsingham, Norfolk (B1105 4m.n. of Fakenham)   While it is still an important place of pilgrimage, in the Middle Ages Walsingham drew pilgrims from all over Europe. At Houghton St Giles a mile to the south is the restored Slipper Chapel.

Central and southern England

Binsey, Oxford (1½m.n.-w. of Oxford city centre)   In the churchyard of the quiet hamlet of Binsey, isolated within the Oxford ring road, is a well dedicated to St Margaret and associated with St Frideswide, the saint of Oxford.

Canterbury, Kent   St Augustine arrived here in 597 and converted Ethelbert, king of Kent, in his capital. Its claim to primacy dates from the time when Augustine was created archbishop. The sanctity of Canterbury was later enhanced by Lanfranc, the first Norman archbishop, and then by the martyrdom of Thomas à Becket. The choir of the cathedral dates from the outset of English Gothic, and its nave is one of its last and greatest glories.

Gloucester, Gloucs   Gloucester became a place of pilgrimage when the abbey accepted the body of the murdered King Edward II, and the income derived from the pilgrims provided for the rebuilding of the choir and the cloisters. The cathedral has a massively monumental nave, a pioneering Perpendicular choir, and the richest of cloisters.

Hailes, Gloucs (e. of A46, 3m.n.-e. of Winchcombe)   Hailes Abbey was Cistercian, founded in 1246 by Richard, Earl of Cornwall, after he had escaped drowning in a shipwreck. In 1270 the abbey was given a phial containing drops of Holy Blood (guaranteed by the Patriarch of Jerusalem), and this brought many pilgrims. The setting is beautiful, though the ruins are scanty.

Hereford, Hereford & Worcs   The founding of Hereford is associated with the murder by King Offa of Æthelberht, king of East Anglia, in 793, after which miracles were said to take place at his tomb. The cathedral has suffered more alteration than most in recent centuries. It is attractively situated and is distinguished by a rigorously geometrical north transept.

Jordans, Bucks (3m.e. of Beaconsfield, n. of A40)   At Old Jordans there is a late 17th-century Quaker meeting-house, a barn built from the timbers of the *Mayflower* and a centre run by the Society of Friends, all most beautiful and emanating a deep sense of peace.

Kilpeck, Hereford & Worcs (8m.s.-w. of Hereford, 1m.s. of A465)   Probably the outstanding Norman parish church in Britain, this is a tiny three-cell building of Old Red sandstone, with unique and extensive carving.

Oxford, Oxon   The cathedral is tiny, shortened by the later building of Tom quad in Christ Church College. Previously the abbey church of St Frideswide, it is a Norman building of original design with a choir vault of intricate richness.

Rollright Stones, Oxon (4m.n. of Chipping Norton, just w. of A361)   A circle of particularly gnarled stones, with an outlying stone and a burial chamber quite nearby.

St Albans, Herts   Verulamium is famous as a Roman city, but the site was occupied long before in prehistoric times. Roman Christianity produced England's first martyr, St Alban, to whom the abbey was dedicated. The great church is of particular interest for its early Norman architecture.

Shoreham, Kent (just w. of A225, 5m.n. of Sevenoaks)   Shoreham was the village of Samuel Palmer, and the gentle scenery of the Darent valley was the inspiration for his visionary paintings.

Silchester, Hants (2m.n. of Basingstoke on A340; e. for 5m. along unclassified road)   Except for the perimeter wall the Roman city is buried, but a grid pattern can be discerned from the air, and there is a strong atmosphere of the past.

Sinodun Hills, Oxon (s. of Dorchester-on-Thames, 1m.n.-w. of Brightwell)   The trees on these two gentle hills overlooking the Thames are known as the Wittenham Clumps. On one, Castle Hill, is a simple Iron Age hillfort called Sinodun Camp.

Uffington, Oxon (6m.w. of Wantage, just s. of B4507)   The famous White Horse, an impressive turf-cut figure, resembles the horse on late Iron Age coins. The best impression is from the far distance: it is about 360ft long. Below the horse is Dragon Hill, where St George is said to have killed the dragon.

Wayland's Smithy, Oxon (1m.s.-w. of **Uffington White Horse** on Ridgeway)   A burial mound of unique interest, it contains chambers of two periods, the earlier of wood, the later of stone. The name comes from the legendary smith of the Saxon gods.

Westminster, London   Westminster Abbey is one of the most visited places in Britain, with very many historical associations binding it to the spirit of the nation. The architecture is quite splendid, with many French influences; Henry VII's Chapel is a pinnacle of the English Gothic.

White Tower, London   William the Conqueror's castle, the Tower of London, was one of the elements of his stabilization programme after the Conquest. The White Tower has a primitive Norman chapel which shows the beginnings of an architectural tradition extending to the present.

Wilmington, Sussex (2m.w. of Polegate just s. of A27)   The Long Man of Wilmington is a slender turf-cut figure with a staff in each hand. He is dated to the 7th century AD and might originally have represented Woden with two spears.

Wales

Anglesey, Gwynedd   The island of Anglesey, separated by the

Menai Strait from the mountains of Snowdonia to the south-east, was sacred to the Druids, whose practices were so degenerate by the time the Romans arrived that the latter made a point of stamping them out. Anglesey is rich in megalithic remains.

Bardsey Island, Gwynedd (2 m. s.-w. of tip of Lleyn Peninsula) Bardsey, the 'Isle of Twenty Thousand Saints', was an important place of pilgrimage in the Middle Ages. It is also one of the legendary resting-places of Merlin. Now it is a bird sanctuary.

Bryn-celli-ddu, Anglesey, Gwynedd (2 m. s.-w. of Menai bridge off A4080) This is a quite exceptional burial chamber, and in very good condition. It has a patterned stone suggesting an association with New Grange in Ireland, and shows signs of having been ceremonially erected on a demolished stone circle, apparently the sign of a clash of cultures.

Holywell, Clwyd (on A55 between Chester and Colwyn Bay) Holywell is the only shrine in Britain with a history of pilgrimage continuous from the Middle Ages to the present. St Winifred's Well is located in the undercroft of a chapel built 1490–1500. It is a healing well, and beside it used to lie a heap of abandoned crutches.

Llanthony Abbey, Gwent (on B4423, 11 m. n. of Abergavenny) The Abbey was built in this remote but very impressive location as a result of the conversion of William de Lacy, who sheltered there in an old chapel in the late 11th century. The buildings and their setting are very picturesque, and of some architectural interest.

Penmon Priory, Anglesey, Gwynedd (at e. extremity of Anglesey) The priory is reputed to have been founded in the 6th century. Near the church is St Seiriol's well beside a low cliff, a place with a wonderful atmosphere of tranquillity.

Pentre Ifan, Dyfed (2 m. s. of A487, 9 m. s.-w. of Cardigan) This dramatic megalith, the denuded stones of a burial chamber, is one of the best known in Wales, set in a lovely valley with views down to the sea.

Prescelly Mountains, Dyfed (e. of Fishguard) These are the hills from which the bluestone uprights of Stonehenge were brought in the Bronze Age, and since this was realized only in this century, the old legend that Stonehenge, the Giants' Dance, was brought by Merlin from the west, Ireland in the story, becomes all the more significant.

Priestholm, Anglesey, Gwynedd (off e. tip of Anglesey) This island, also known as Puffin Island, is another sacred to a Celtic saint, St Seiriol, and there are some remains. The island should perhaps be renamed for it is now overrun with rats, which have reduced the bird population and dangerously tunnelled the ground surface.

St David's Cathedral, Dyfed The premier cathedral of Wales, built on the site of the 6th-century church of St David. It is a church with a variety of interesting features. The charming little city of St Davids makes an attractive setting.

St Govan's Chapel, Dyfed (at St Govan's Head, directly s. of Pembroke) In this romantic spot the little chapel nestles into the cliffs. There is an interesting association with the Arthurian knight Gawain.

Strata Florida Abbey, Dyfed (e. of B4343, 18 m. s.-e. of Aberystwyth) This was a Cistercian foundation, and apparently typical in its layout, although the remains are scanty apart from the splendid west door. Strata Florida became an important centre of national culture for Wales.

Tintern Abbey, Gwent (A466 between Chepstow and Monmouth) A Cistercian house in what was then an austere setting, Tintern now presents a combination of outstanding location in the glorious valley of the Wye, architectural splendour, and intensely romantic associations.

Valle Crucis Abbey, Clwyd (nr A542, 2 m. n. of Llangollen) Another Cistercian abbey, Valle Crucis is charmingly enclosed by hills, but unfortunately also often surrounded by caravans. The abbey is small, with a picturesque west front

and a well-preserved chapter-house.

Whitesand Bay, Dyfed (just w. of St Davids) This is the broad sandy bay, overlooked by St David's Head, from which St Patrick is reputed to have set sail for Ireland. It is now a popular beach.

Scotland

Aberlemno, Tayside (B9134, 5 m. n.-e. of Forfar) Two splendid Pictish crosses, one in the churchyard and one by the roadside, show the unusual combination of Christian symbols on one side and enigmatic pagan symbols on the other.

Birsay, Orkney (tidal island off n.-w. tip of Mainland) Fragments of an early Christian church and a number of Norse houses stand on this rocky little island, their beautifully coloured sandstone contrasting with the delicate Orkney sky.

Brodgar, Orkney (on Mainland, n.-w. of A965 Stromness to Finstown) Without doubt one of the most beautiful and haunting of British stone circles, very large, with tall slabs set overlooking water on each side of a narrow strip of land.

Callanish, Isle of Lewis (just off A858, 15 m. w. of Stornoway) The standing stones of Callanish rank among the most impressive and moving of megalithic monuments in Britain, and are all the more affecting since so few people visit them. The complex consists of a cross and a circle of slender glittering white stones. It appears to have a significant lunar association. In the past, legend maintained that those who were not meant to see it would be prevented.

Dryburgh Abbey, Borders (3 m. s.-e. of Melrose, nr St Boswells) Each of the Border abbeys has its own quality, and Dryburgh is notable for its delightful woodland setting. It was an abbey of Premonstratensian canons, and is the burial-place of Sir Walter Scott.

Dunfermline Abbey, Fife (A823 off M90) This abbey of Benedictine monks became one of the richest in Scotland, and had considerable royal connections, with an adjacent palace and many royal burials including Robert the Bruce. The nave piers are patterned in the same way as the Durham piers.

Dunadd Fort, Argyll, Strathclyde (just w. of A816, 5 m. n. of Lochgilphead) Dunadd was the capital of Dalriada. It is a walled fort on an isolated hilltop, in an area rich in interest.

Egilsay, Orkney (an island 12 m. n. of Kirkwall) A boat trip from Mainland to Rousay and Egilsay is well worth while. On Egilsay are the remains of the church of St Magnus, with its round tower, rather Irish in style, close to the place of St Magnus' martyrdom.

Glasgow Cathedral, Strathclyde Glasgow Cathedral is far less well known than it deserves to be; it is a quite splendid example of early Gothic, subtly different from contemporary English churches. The blackened stonework of the exterior provides a majestic silhouette.

Holyrood Abbey, Edinburgh, Lothian Holyrood, palace and abbey, stands at the east end of Edinburgh's Royal Mile. Of the abbey only the ruined nave remains, a very fine design, with a notable west front.

Inchcolm Abbey, Firth of Forth, Fife (4 m. e. of Forth Bridges) Inchcolm, 'the Iona of the East', is a remarkably complete abbey complex, protected by its island situation, even today, for it has recently become difficult to obtain a boat passage.

Iona, Strathclyde (island w. of Mull: frequent ferries from Fionnphort, A849) Few people sensitive to atmosphere who have visited Iona could fail to place it very high among the holy places of Britain. It is a place with a strong spiritual quality. Here in 563 St Columba founded the monastery, and there are many other buildings and ruins, all deeply moving.

Jedburgh Abbey, Borders (A68, 11 m. n. of border) The abbey, which faces away from the town, is a large, mainly Romanesque church, with much of architectural interest.

Kintraw, Argyll, Strathclyde (A816 between Lochgilphead and Oban) The cairns and standing stone at Kintraw have been important in Professor Thom's thesis on the astronomical basis of some megalithic sites, and it seems unlikely that any such use was separate from religious practices.

Kirkwall, Orkney (principal town of Orkney islands, on Mainland) The two major towns of Orkney, Kirkwall and Stromness, have a different atmosphere from any other British towns. They are paved in the sandstone that has been such a gift to the people of Orkney from the prehistoric period to the present. Kirkwall Cathedral is a red sandstone church, mainly Romanesque, but showing a remarkably smooth transition in style to Gothic over the decades of its building.

Maeshowe, Orkney (on Mainland, beside A965 between Stromness and Finstown) This is the best chambered tomb in Britain, built of the Orkney sandstone that finishes to a remarkably rectangular shape, so that the interior is the most regular of all such tombs. The Viking graffiti inside comprise the largest collection of runic inscriptions in Europe.

Melrose Abbey, Borders (A6091, 2 m.e. of A68) Melrose is perhaps the most famous of the Border abbeys, a spectacular ruin, and architecturally the most beautiful, with most of the surviving structure dating from a 15th-century rebuilding in elaborate Gothic. The red stone is subtly responsive to changing light, but is best in sunlight against a blue sky.

Roslin Chapel, Lothian (off A701, 8 m.s. of Edinburgh) The chapel is the choir of a collegiate church built in the 15th century. It is decorated with almost unparalleled richness in a fashion unusual in Britain.

Rousay, Orkney (island immediately n. of Mainland: regular ferry service) Rousay is noted for its many, varied, and elaborate chambered tombs, and for the well preserved Mid Howe Broch.

Ruthwell, Dumfries and Galloway (between Carlisle and Dumfries, just s. of B724 6 m.w. of Annan) With the Bewcastle cross, the Ruthwell cross is the best surviving example of the Anglian art of the 7th and 8th centuries, with capable and expressive carving, and inscriptions in Latin and runic characters.

St Andrews, Fife (A91, on coast) St Andrews is a town of exceptional character, with popular, sporting, and cultural associations, as well as a very ancient standing in the religious life of Scotland. The remains of the cathedral are not extensive, but full of atmosphere, and not far away is the older church of St Rule or Regulus.

St Ninian's Cave, Dumfries and Galloway (on coast 3 m.s.-s.-w. of Whithorn on A746) There are the remains of ancient churches at Whithorn and Isle of Whithorn, and a museum of crosses at Whithorn, all associated with St Ninian, who in the 4th century may have brought the first Christian mission to reach Scotland, but it is the cave he used that now holds the most pervasive air of sanctity.

Skara Brae, Orkney (at Skail, middle of w. coast of Mainland) A Stone Age settlement of truly unexpected sophistication, extending even to stone furniture, Skara Brae can fairly be described as unique. It is possible that it was the home of a dedicated community of a monastic type, perhaps connected with the construction of the megalithic structures round about.

Stenness, Orkney (nr **Maeshowe** and **Brodgar**) The few remaining uprights of a circle thought to be the predecessor of Brodgar. The stones are exceptionally tall and slender.

Sweetheart Abbey, Dumfries and Galloway (A710 7 m.s. of Dumfries) The remains of the lovely red sandstone church stand to roof level, and are of the simple, straightforward style characteristic of the Cistercians.

Ireland

Ahenny, Tipperary (w. of L26, 5 m.n. of Carrick-on-Suir) Two of the finest of Irish high crosses, both dated very early, in the 8th century, and decorated entirely with geometrical ornament,

mainly swirls and spirals, with figures only on the bases.

Annaghdown, Galway (beside L.Corrib 10 m.n. of Galway) There are two sites at Annaghdown, the cathedral and the priory. The cathedral is a roofless shell of 15th-century date, but with a fine 12th-century east window. The Augustinian priory has an almost military feel about it. Annaghdown is in flat countryside by the lough, and has a distinctive atmosphere.

Ardmore, Waterford (south coast, 40 m.e. of Cork) The monastic foundation of Ardmore is believed to date from before the time of St Patrick. The later round tower and cathedral are characteristic of Irish sites. The cathedral has a notable collection of sculpture, in a stone of many subtle colours.

Armagh, Armagh (40 m.s.-w. of Belfast) Armagh has been a centre of Irish Christianity for fifteen centuries, since the foundation of St Patrick's first church on the site of the present (modern) cathedral. The precinct is a haven of calm in a troubled city.

Beaghmore, Tyrone (12 m.w.-n.-w. of Cookstown, n. of A505, nr Dunnamore) A sacred site from Neolithic times, now covered with an unusually concentrated group of Bronze Age circles and alignments. The site was discovered only recently, during peat clearance, and probably extends further under the surrounding peat land.

Carrowmore, Sligo (3 m.s.-s.-w. of Sligo) Carrowmore is one of the most extensive groupings of Neolithic chambered tombs in the British Isles, and it is believed that the remaining tombs are only about a third of the total, many having been lost during gravel working. On Knocknarea not far away is a huge cairn reputed to be the grave of Queen Maeve.

Cashel, Tipperary (13 m.e. of Tipperary) On the Rock of Cashel, inside the great perimeter wall or cashel with its round towers, is a cathedral with a castle built into its nave, and the greatest work of Irish Romanesque, Cormac's Chapel.

Clonfert, Galway (between N62 and T31, 12 m.n.-w. of Birr) The small medieval cathedral at Clonfert is noted for its striking quality of its great west door, with its elaborate arches and gable, supported by oddly slanting columns.

Clonmacnois, Offaly (13 m.e. of Ballinasloe via L27) Clonmacnois, like other early monastic sites in Ireland, possesses several churches, including a cathedral. The precinct, with its churches, towers, and crosses, lies on a sloping hillside by the Shannon, and it has a haunting beauty.

Corcomroe Abbey, Clare (nr N67, s. of Burren, 27 m.s. of Galway) This was a Cistercian house, of which the modest church is the principal remnant. The choir is notable, with fine masonry and carving.

Croagh Patrick, Mayo (s. of Murrisk, 6 m.w. of Westport) This is St Patrick's Holy Mountain, a 2500-ft quartzite cone, with a long history of pilgrimage which is very much alive today. The climb is a worthwhile experience which offers rewards in any weather.

Drombeg Stone Circle, Cork (nr L191 between Glandore and Ross Carbery) This is a small circle, but with substantial stones closely spaced, so that it offers a good impression of this type of monument. It has a portal and a recumbent stone on the same axis, aligned with the winter solstice sunset. There is a later habitation site nearby.

Dublin, Dublin A city with two medieval cathedrals, Christ Church and St Patrick's. Both are early Gothic designs, and both have been subjected to much restoration and rebuilding (especially Christ Church), but nevertheless they retain the Gothic power to affect the visitor.

Glendalough, Wicklow (4 m.w. of T61, directly w. of Wicklow) The monastic site at Glendalough is one of the most extensive in Ireland, with several churches and other monuments, all spread out over a large area in a lovely valley. Perhaps most interesting is the stone-roofed church of St Kevin, built in fact long after his death.

Holy Cross Abbey, Tipperary (on N62 between Cashel and

Thurles)   Recently restored, Holy Cross is one of the finest of late medieval churches in Ireland. The chancel and transepts were built in the 15th century, of smooth grey stone, elegantly designed and decorated.

Inishcaeltra, Clare (island on Lough Derg, near Mountshannon, accessible by boat from nearby jetty)   This low-lying island holds the ruins of an early Christian monastery, with several churches and a round tower. It became a place of pilgrimage, and now, isolated and deserted, it is pervaded by a reflective quiet.

Inishmurray, Sligo (island – 10m. by boat, hired at Mullaghmore)   Inishmurray is 4 miles out into the Atlantic, and has been deserted for over 30 years. The departed community had, for practical and superstitious reasons, preserved intact through the centuries a 6th-century monastic site of quite exceptional importance, and it is now by far the best place to obtain an impression of the nature of the holy sites of this important period of Irish Christianity.

Jerpoint Abbey, Kilkenny (on N9, just s. of Thomastown)   The church, cloister, and monastic buildings are well preserved; this is one of the best of Ireland's Cistercian ruins.

Kildare, Kildare (on N7, 33m.s.-w. of Dublin)   The cathedral is on an early site, with a fine round tower. The battlemented church is much restored, but it conveys a good impression of the character of the time, and has fine monuments.

Kilkenny, Kilkenny   As well as three medieval monastic sites, Kilkenny possesses a cathedral which is among the finest in Ireland, beautifully located, architecturally and spatially rich, and well endowed with interesting tombs.

Killaloe, Clare (15m.n.-n.-e. of Limerick)   The cathedral and the older stone-roofed oratory of St Flannan stand beside the smooth-flowing Shannon. The plastered choir, with its attenuated eastern lancets, has a cool serenity.

Kilmacduagh, Clare (on L55, 3m.s.-w. of Gort, 24m.s. of Galway)   This isolated site is surrounded by the amazing stony landscape and hills of the Burren, with the ruined churches and the leaning tower idyllic against the constantly changing Irish sky.

Lough Derg, Donegal (e. of Donegal, on L84 n. from Pettigo)   An island on this lough contains the lost site of St Patrick's Purgatory, a cave in which the saint experienced the three worlds of the after-life. The island is now covered by a great basilica, and is still a place of pilgrimage and retreat.

Lough Gur, Limerick (e. of T50A, 15m.s. of Limerick)   The land around Lough Gur is the most important locality in Ireland for the study of prehistory. It has numerous habitation sites, several excellent stone circles, and a good information centre for visitors.

Mellifont Abbey, Louth (s. of T25, 7m.n.-w. of Drogheda)   This Cistercian abbey has lost most of its church, but retains a vaulted chapter-house, and, more unusually, part of an octagonal lavabo in the cloister.

Monasterboice, Louth (w. of T1, 7m.n. of Drogheda)   Muiredach's Cross at Monasterboice is regarded as the finest of the high crosses of the Irish tradition. It is dated from the 8th or 9th century, and is elaborately carved with biblical and other figures.

There is a second cross almost as fine, and part of a third, as well as the remains of two churches and a round tower.

New Grange, Louth (6m.w. of Drogheda, by N51)   This is the finest of all Neolithic chambered tombs, vast in size, rich in carving, with a very clear solar alignment, and now daringly restored with a steep wall finished in white quartzite stones. It is one of three notable chambered tombs in the area.

Quin, Clare (8m.e.-s.-e. of Ennis)   Quin is one of many surviving Franciscan friaries in Ireland. It has the usual simple church, slender tower with stepped battlements, and an enclosed miniature cloister, but it has also the unusual feature of having been built in the remains of a bastioned castle.

Ross Erilly, Galway (e. of Lough Corrib near Headford, 17m.n. of Galway)   One of the most characteristic of the Franciscan friaries of Ireland, isolated, severe, but moving in its harmony with the landscape, Ross Erilly Friary continued in use well into the 18th century.

Scattery, Clare (island in Shannon: access by boat hired at Kilrush)   This is another of the early Christian monastic sites with several churches and a round tower. The island is unoccupied, and the ruins are seen in a state of ideal purity, separated from the everyday world, under the great hemisphere of the Shannon estuary sky.

Skellig Michael, Kerry (island 8m.w. of Bolus Head: access by daily boats from Portmagee, in fine weather)   The island mountain of Skellig Michael, with its outstanding early Christian monastery, is one of the great sights in the whole of the British Isles. The whole trip there and the climb to the top is something of a pilgrimage even today, while the view from the top, with the monastery perched on its ledge, the sea, Little Skellig, and the distant mainland, is breathtaking.

Slane, Meath (9m.w. of Drogheda, on M51)   The hill of Slane is where St Patrick is said to have kindled the first Paschal fire in Ireland, to the confusion of the High King and his druids. The hill and its ruins retain a magical quality.

Tara, Meath (nr N3, 7m.s.-s.-e. of Navan)   This is the ancient royal seat of Ireland, and the focal point for many heroic tales of Irish folklore. The remains are mostly earthworks, with the Stone of Destiny or royal inauguration stone as a focal point. The views are memorable.

Timoleague, Cork (L42, 6m.e. of Clonakilty)   Although the Franciscan friary was founded on an early monastic site, the ruins are of the 14th and 15th centuries, with a conspicuous tower. The friary is beautifully situated near the sea.

Turoe Stone, Galway (nr Bullaun on L11, 3m.n. of Loughrea, e. of Galway)   A squat upright pillar of granite, rounded and carved with elaborate swirls of relief decoration in the La Tène style of Celtic art of the centuries before the Christian era.

White Island, Fermanagh (island on Lower Lough Erne, s. of Kesh)   Built into the ruined church on this island is a remarkable collection of early sculptures, grotesque figures assumed to have been taken from an earlier church. They imply a local tradition of sculpture, probably with pagan roots.

Index

Entries in bold type refer to plate numbers